SPIRAL TO ECONOMIC DISASTER

***

LIFEBOAT MEASURES - IF YOU ACT NOW

BY

GYEORGOS CERES HATONN

"DHARMA"

Library of Congress Cataloging-in-Publication Data

First Edition Printed by America West Distributors, 1989

Published by

AMERICA WEST DISTRIBUTORS
6992 El Camino Real #104-335
Carlsbad, California 92009
Printed in the United States of America
10 9 8 7 6 5 4 3 2 1

The people and groups to which I refer in this document, or any other, does not necessarily represent the opinions of the ones involved. I have chosen their material and services because it is valid and honest in a most dishonest environment. There are portions of all programs and books with which we of these higher realms do not agree. Please utilize the information with discernment and gracious honor unto the ones who have cared enough about you, the people, to publicly give forth their ideas and services. In the instance of Dr. John King, it is his preference to not endorse this material. Those who wish to avail themselves of his services (which I most heartily endorse), may gain information by contacting A.S.S.K. or Mr. E.J. Ekker as referenced in the Appendix relative to Mr. Laughlin. The addition of addresses and business phone numbers in no way reflects to them personally. I place them there for convenience to those of you who desire truth and are seeking solutions to very critical circumstances. I repeat, THESE ARE MY RECOMMENDATIONS AND IN NO WAY REFLECT THE OPINIONS OF THOSE MENTIONED WITHIN THESE DOCUMENTS. I HONOR THEIR PRIVACY AND FURTHER, I GIVE CREDIT FOR EXCEPTIONAL CONTRIBUTION TO THEIR FELLOWMAN. HATONN

TABLE OF CONTENTS

REC #1, HATONN

FRIDAY, SEPTEMBER 1, 1989 6:30 A.M. YEAR 3, DAY 016

INTRODUCTION

You can separate your man-doctrined "churches" (cults) from your state---you have. Then you can separate the true church of God from those---which you have! Then your house of cards will fall---which it is! Those of you on Earth who truly place your lives on the basis of truth, love of God, love of The Creation, and love of your fellow man are all but negligible. Those who tout to do so are false and have forgotten the true Laws of The Creation and God. It has come its full cycle, just as prophesied, to smite you down. Bit by bit your world is coming down like the reverse pyramid--built on the point and the point is blown away---it will crush you all. YOU HAVE LOST YOUR WAY.

I see no way for you to get the whole tapestry without all the documents we will provide for you. In this one, I will duplicate what we refer to as the "Grey Men" document. I am requesting that it be placed in the near beginning of this document compilation. You must know how bad it is in order to take me seriously enough to take action.

I am greatly indebted to ones who do not yet even know of me. I honor them and I dedicate this "LIFEBOAT" to them. Honor them, oh peoples of these wondrous United States of America, for if you survive at all, it will be because of ones such as these. Dr. JOHN L. KING, HARLEY LAUGHLIN, MERLIN B. SAMPSON. THEY HAVE GIVEN GREATLY OF THEMSELVES THAT YOU MIGHT HAVE SOME MEASURE OF A CHANCE AT SURVIVAL. WE OF THESE REALMS DO SALUTE THEM.

In Dr. King's words, you are "Running on empty..." It is far worse than that, friends, for when the vehicle ceases to run you have no-where to go to get more fuel.

This document is offered in response to ones who continue to ask me, "When?" and "What do we do?". In an economic vein, it has gone beyond the ability to reverse it, therefore, it will have to pass through the equalizer of collapse. I only present possible ways to salvage your stability on a personal basis FOR IT <u>WILL</u> ALL FALL DOWN AROUND YOU. <u>ALL</u> HAS PASSED BEYOND YOUR ABILITY TO REVERSE IT---YOU ARE IN THE ENDING TIMES, UPON A PLANET IN REBIRTHING AND REBERTHING INTO A HIGHER EXISTENCE. YOU HAVE REACHED THE TIME OF ARMAGEDDON!

I only deal with the United States in this particular discourse, for this is where my assignment predominantly places me in this Earth commission. I cover very little history as to how your world arrived at this financial disaster for I wish to give you something to actively undertake--history is history, you need guidance NOW! There is already abundance of history from which you did not learn, let us walk as many as possible through this mire.

I request that my credentials be placed at the rear of this ledger that you can recognize of me. (Please see EPILOGUE.)

I come in truth, directly from your Creator Source. I serve in the immediate Command of the one you call "Jesus", Esu Immanuel (His name) Sananda ("and He shall bear a new name at the time of His return"). Discount it if you choose. Be most careful, however, for your days upon this orb are numbered within thy accounting ability. These things of which the prophets wrote, will come upon you within this generation of your elderly ones. All the signs are in place, dear ones. We are all in service to our Cosmic Universe, Sananda and Creator Aton of the Total Light; God and The Creation which is above all. We also come in service and love unto you ones to assist you through the times of tribulations and bring you home.

He went forth before you to prepare a place for you. He has done so----are you ready? We now prepare you to receive of Him that you be not frightened. He (Immanuel Sananda), is come to bring you home, those of his flock. Galactic fleets stand ready to take you up. HOW DID YOU THINK HE WOULD COME?

Those who choose to remain in ignorance of truth, will not be coerced in any manner. 'Tis thy choice all the way to the gate. Choose to continue as you are and you will spend a very long time with the false teachers who have led you down this tacky roadway---however, it has been your free-will choice to follow them.

HOW DID YOU BELIEVE HIS RETURN WOULD BE?

OH BELOVED ONES, TO SIT ON SOME MISERABLE CLOUD BANKS WITH HIM IS FOOLISH THOUGHT INDEED. THOSE CLOUDS YOU SEE ARE IN YOUR ATMOSPHERE WHICH WILL PROBABLY BE FILLED WITH RADIATION AND DEATH. THE MASTER WOULD NOT PLACE YOU THERE. YOU WILL BE TAKEN UP INTO CRAFT, THOSE OF YOU WHO ARE PREPARED, AND INTO SAFETY. THE TRANSITION WILL BE MOST HARD ON YOUR PHYSICAL BODIES--TO CHANGE DIMENSION SO RAPIDLY. <u>PLEASE START THY PETITIONS FOR INSTRUCTION AND RECEIVE OF THAT WHICH IS GIVEN UNTO YOU BY US THROUGH THESE SCRIBES AND RECEIVERS.</u> MAKE SURE THE RECEIVERS ARE OF THE LIGHTED REALMS FOR THE DARK BROTHERHOOD OF SATANIC FORCES OVERTAKE YOU AT EVERY TURN. THEY HAVE ALL BUT DESTROYED YOU AS A CIVILIZATION. THEY MAY VERY WELL ANNIHILATE YOU IF YOU DO NOT TURN ABOUT INTO TRUTH. SO BE IT, BELOVED BROTHERS, FOR THE TIME IS AT HAND. AMEN, AND UPON THIS I PLACE MY SEAL OF TRUTH AND HONOR.

MAY YOU SEEK TRUTH IN THY GOD AND CREATION FOR THY WAY IS HARD.
MAY YE FIND PEACE WITHIN. I AM HATONN

CHAPTER 1

REC #1, HATONN

TUESDAY, AUGUST 29, 1989 6:30 A.M. YEAR 3, DAY 013

Thank you, Dharma. Greetings in the Light of the Radiant One. Let us speak today on the coming depression and ultimate collapse of your monetary system.

You ones are going to have to live with repetition, in some instances, from document to document. There is no other way to get information to those who will pick up a book without having read its predecessor. Today, we will organize the probable outlay so that information is understandable but brief enough that man can "act" instead of sit and contemplate his plight. I will get to the point first, then tell you a bit about "why".

ECONOMIC SEERS OF TODAY

I will tell you right up front, with no equivocation, that everyone who hears me should be looking for guidance from one on your place. I scan and find this is the only one I feel is so accurate that I counsel you to carefully give ear.

The great majority of "economic" advisers are incorrect. Some who are most outstanding and well received in the crowd of self-proclaimed experts are set up to distract and mislead you.

I will only take one as explanation to the above statement. Whether he wittingly or unwittingly participates in the plan of deception is of no real concern. He does, however, give the exact information the government and "gray men" bankers, CIA, etc. desire you to have. Leading you right down the path of the sheep trail. These ones give one or two tidbits of true advice (which was set and told to them in advance), suck you in and then blow you out. I would remind you ones that Mr. Mark Skousen, for instance, was a major player within the ranks of the CIA and touts his "inside" information as a bonus for you. It would be, if you were able to discern truth.

Let me read you a few "headings" from his current bulletin. "Outlook Bright for Traditional Investment Markets", "Stock Market Headed for New Highs", etc. Actually, portions of the report itself are accurate, other portions of his letter are even more accurate, but can you as a little citizen, understand which is which? He touts "Super Speculation in S&L's"; well, that is exactly what it sounds like, speculation, because your

S&L bailout was the starting gun of the marathon to doom.

As instruction, Dharma, for the placement of writings for this document, I request that the section from "Space-Gate" be placed right up front. You ones need to know the actions of the ones who control you, that you might understand what is happening here.

Right up front, also, I would urge Oberli to get in touch with one known in business as E.J. Ekker in California. I will be giving information from some of your Earth publications which are superb tools for you ones and I do not wish to give forth unpermitted information as to resource. I would ask please that I be allowed to give Mr. Ekker's address for requested material and he can either make arrangements to ship requested material, or, forward the order requests.

I would like it known that what I will give you is totally credible and I also give credit for truth to those who speak truth.

One such is Dr. John King. He has a News service to which ones can subscribe for $59.00. (Three months trial is about $20.00). He also has a book which will move right along with my explanations, called PROFIT FROM THE NEXT GREAT DEPRESSION. There are several other similar booklets but I scan and pronounce that Dr. King's is outstanding. Not a pretty picture; but truth.

I will also be suggesting Nevada based corporations. Therefore ones need a place to receive the Corporation Manual of Harley Laughlin, as well as how, who, where etc., of incorporating. Please check and see how much Mr. Ekker is willing to handle from his business office. I apologize for utilizing willing hands to overburden, but we must allow the public to have the information. I can be of no real help to you ones if I only give you spiritual pats upon your backs and say "there, there". My commitment is to help in a very physical manner, where I can do so. My primary commitment, however, is to keep my receivers and workers in total safety that our work is not interrupted.

If it is permissible with Mr. Ekker, you will please give forth addresses etc. and delete whatever is necessary from this writing for final printing.

THE SECRET GOVERNMENT

As you ones will see after reading my outline of the "gray men" banking structure you will better understand all the picture. I highly recommend my prior book, "SPACE-GATE" for I carefully explain how important the Secret "Supra-Government" truly is. I especially emphasize the Council on Foreign Relations. I am going to shock you here by just listing, in paragraph format, some major, major participants. It will not be current for so many ones have merged and integrated that it would take volumes to include all fragments.

All banking, all major publication publishers, all major public information (poll) services and all major foundations, as well as major networks and businesses are members of the Council on Foreign Relations. That would seem to be a good thing; not so! You are controlled and headed for economic slavery, bankruptcy and world control by less than fourteen "families".

CFR members, and this is but a brief, brief highlight listing: Money: Kuhn Loeb, Lazard Freres, DillonRead, Lehman Bros., Goldman-Sachs, Chase Manhattan, Chemical, Irving Trust, Castle bank and its holding companies, Asian Development Bank, the Nugan Han Banks and holding companies, J. Henry Schroder Banking Corp., Schroder Trust Co., Schroders Limited (London), Shroder Gerbruder and Co. (Germany), Schroder Munchmeyer Hengst & Co., Federal Reserve, and, and, and.

Media: NBC, CBS, Time, Life, Fortune, Look, Newsweek, New York Times, Washington Post, L.A. Times, New York Post, McGraw-Hill, Simon & Shuster, Harper Bros., Book of the Month, Saturday Review, Business Week and, and, and. PERHAPS YOU MIGHT NOW UNDERSTAND WHY WE DO NOT WANT ANYTHING TO DO WITH THESE PUBLISHERS. ALL YOU RECEIVE IS APPROVED AND WRITTEN DIRECTLY FOR YOUR BLIND CONSUMPTION. WE HAVE TO CHOOSE WHAT YOU CALL AN "EGO PRESS" TO EVEN GET THIS INFORMATION TO YOU, THE PUBLIC. SO BE IT.

Further now, your entire Executive Department of the Government are members. All your major Foundations, Rockefeller, Ford, and Carnegie. Also your major institutes of study and research, Rand, Hudson Institute, Fund for the Republic and Brookings Institute. And, well, lets name a few companies on the "in and on it list": Standard Oil, Shell Oil (well, all the oil magnates except the independent ones who got set up and "done in" in Texas), IBM, Xerox, Eastman Kodak, Pan American, Firestone, U.S. Steel, and, and, and.

Now, who do you think has controlled the Political Parties? Ah, I thought you might be getting the picture. There is a perfectly controlled and managed news and information curtain. I am only going to list up to and including Hubert Humphrey (whose soul probably does not rest in such great peace) and Richard Nixon, for the remainder I have included in my aforementioned writings.

Democrats: Dean Acheson, Alger Hiss, Adlai Stevenson, John Kennedy, Edward Kennedy, Robert Kennedy, Averell Harriman, George Ball, Henry Fowler, Dean Rusk, Adam Yarmolinsky, John K. Galbraith, Arthur Schlesinger, Jr., Hubert Humphrey and John Lindsay.

And now, equal time to the Republicans: Dwight Eisenhower, John Foster Dulles, Thomas E. Dewey, Jacob Javits, Paul Hoffman, Robert McNamara, John Gardner, Henry Cabot Lodge, Rockefellers (all), Elliott Richardson, Arthur Burns, Henry Kissinger and Richard Nixon.

I am sure it becomes most clear to you what might stop any outside candidate from even getting audience! Further, after they push their way on through to the public, they later end up in jail or broken following the political show every four years. OH, BLIND LITTLE LAMBS, WAKE UP; PLEASE WAKE UP. THE TRAITORS TO YOU AND YOUR BLESSED COUNTRY ARE IN POWER, DO YOU NOT SEE? TO "QUESTION" IS NOT TO BE A TRAITOR; TO "NOT QUESTION AND ACT" IS BEING THE TRAITOR FOR YOUR BLESSED COUNTRY HAS BEEN STOLEN FROM YOU, THE PEOPLE, WHO FOUNDED THIS WONDROUS REPUBLIC.

PERHAPS NONE ON YOUR PLACE WILL LABEL THE CONSPIRACY FOR WHAT IT IS. I DARE, FOR YOU HAVE REQUESTED THAT YOU BE GIVEN ASSISTANCE AND IT IS THROUGH GOD'S RESPONSE THAT WE HAVE COME INTO YOUR SPACE. WE HAVE NAUGHT TO GAIN EXCEPT PERHAPS PEACE IN OUR COSMIC SPACE AND TO RECLAIM THAT WHICH IS GOD'S AND THE CHILDREN OF TRUTH AS RELATIVE TO THE PROPHECIES.

CREDENTIALS

I request hereby, that my credentials be published on the opening pages of this document that there be no misunderstanding of my credentials nor who I am. (Please see EPILOGUE.) I write in no particularly acceptable format; I give it to you as it is in hopefully, understandable, blunt terminology. I do not speak English well, I need not speak at all at any time for my communication is of thought vibrational patterns. Do not err by discounting me or my brothers from the Intergalactic environs who have been summoned at this time of transition.

I care not for your formal publication formats. I bring forth truth just as through radio signals and frequencies. My scribes hold no knowledge of Earth workings any more than the most ignorant picking up this material. Yes, afterwards, they are most informed for I insure they come into understanding. There is a chance of the public coming into understanding if I can see that my scribes and receivers comprehend to a great measure. I will never endanger any one of them by allowing prior information nor full understanding. If that were allowed, they would be assassinated immediately. Dharma does not understand the mechanism here, she has only agreed to write. Numerous attempts have been made against her life-----but she is within our protection.

The end times are most near beloved brothers, most near. You have much, much to learn. For instance, how many of you realize that Immanuel was not birthed on December 25th. (A great person was, however, by the name of Isaac Newton). IMMANUEL WAS BORN ON AN AUGUST DAY, COUNTED AS 22. (To some of our most beloved humans, the number 22 will be most important as a spiritual base point.)

You are on the very edge of the abyss. I see not how you can even move into your year 1990 without a major recession and more likely, a full blown depression that will reach proportions as you have never dreamed. You will be protected somewhat in the early onset while the government and banks get in final control. But it is here, brothers, right upon you.

TO SAVE YOURSELVES

There are some measures you might take to assist you in a personal way and thus the purpose for this document.

Your market is ready to totally collapse; get out of it. You are stuck between the proverbial rock and a very hard place. Gold is an excellent choice but take great care; it can be, and will be, confiscated, safe deposit boxes will be frozen, bank accounts frozen, limits on withdrawals will be enacted and enforced, etc. I will give you reasons and "Proof" (it has been done to you prior to this). CASH IS YOUR BEST PLOY. GET AS MUCH AS YOU CAN OUT OF YOUR BANKS IN SMALL BILLS (NO GREATER IN SINGLE BILL SIZE OF $20) AND I PAIN TO SAY THIS, BUT HIDE IT. GET AND KEEP A FULL 30 DAY SUPPLY OF FUNDS, 3 MONTHS IF AT ALL POSSIBLE. YOU ARE GOING TO BE HIT VERY, VERY HARD. DO NOT BE CARELESS HOW YOU HIDE IT FOR YOU WILL NEED IT.

YOUR CURRENCY WILL, HOWEVER, BE DECLARED INVALID AND WORTHLESS AT SOME POINT NOT TOO FAR DISTANT AND WILL BE REPLACED WITH A "NEW" CURRENCY. (DO ANY OF YOU REMEMBER HOW WORTHLESS CONFEDERATE MONEY BECAME?) SO BE IT! YOU WILL THEN HAVE A REPLACEMENT DEBIT CARD SYSTEM COME FORTH AND THEN YOU WILL HAVE WITNESSED THE BEAST IN FULL ARRAY.

I would close now, Dharma, and organize a bit. I am thinking it might be good to start at the present and work backward with explanation. I further would like you ones to council and perhaps we could issue this in an emergency format in two "volumes". I fear the time is so close that it could be too late for the upstart protection, but could help ones see what to do next. Let us decide that early on for it makes a difference in how I require Dharma's hands to be utilized.

Unfortunately, you need all this information AT ONCE, AND BEFORE NOW, but no=one would have listened to me. Who would have listened to a space cadet? Well, I think you are ready to understand that I know of that which I speak for the symptoms and signs are about to bury you. So be it and I place the seal of truth upon the words. Also, I place the shield of protection around you ones who reach out to your fellow man with such dangerous information.

I AM COMMANDER GYEORGOS CERES HATONN. SALU, SALU, SALU

Frequency cleared, Hatonn out please.

CHAPTER 2

THE "GREY MEN" TAPE

This is an edited transcription of a lecture taped April 23, 1988. The information is valid and, if anything, more easily recognized today ---Hatonn.

I will be utiliziing this information again when I speak of economics, but for now, I will modify from the audio tape to save time and repetition.

Let us call the group which has elaborate, and successful, plans to rule your nation and your world, the Internationalists. When I refer to the Internationalists I am referring to a very elite group of about twelve to thirteen "families". These "families" hold your "purse strings"--the zipper and lock, to all the bags of money in your world. Sound impossible? Nay, it is not only possible, it is extremely easy to visualize after I have explained it to you.

As I move along, I will give you some names and places whereby you can check it out on an individual basis. I wish never to place any human at risk, however, so in all instances I will only refer to those already having come forth with "public" statements or information.

I will also have to explain a few terms used to have any sense of continuity. Therefore, as we move along, forgive me of any digression in attempt to give definition, i.e., "fractional banking".

First, you must fully come into understanding that there truly ARE the elite few, with plans well foundationed and functioning, who control both the world financial markets and ultimately will control all peoples of the world. Do not err in your thoughts by thinking I am speaking of "someone else in the world", I speak more for the United States of America than I do of the remainder of your world.

As I pull portions of the puzzle together for this document I shall again be referring to such groups as The Trilateral Commission, the Council on Foreign Relations, and the Bilderburgers. Forgive me if I am repetitious. I may need to be repetitious in order to fit the pieces in proper perspective.

You must know that there are certain families (literally) that control the hard currency. The countries wherein these families abide are known as hard currency countries. These thirteen families have control of the policy making and the decision making of the central banks of those countries. They are owners, these families, of the majority of the stock of the regional banks of the Federal Reserve System. "Federal Reserve" would indicate to the more uninformed, that this is a Federal Governmental Branch. This is untrue, the Federal Reserve System is NOT a branch of your federal government. Just as these families control the regional banks of the Federal Reserve System, they also control the currencies that are not allowed to fluctuate. Note here that the American dollar is the standard against which all other currency is measured. All other nations are affected according to the changing values of the dollar. Not only do these families control the currencies, but they likewise control the banks. This, friends, is in all the leading nations of your world.

For ease of understanding, let us just consider the industrialized nations at this point. I will also need to explain fractional banking to you, because without understanding the lending system you cannot get the picture properly. All of the banks under control of these families practice fractional banking - and beyond - (sometimes there is no hard money present at all). But, let us explain by example on a personal level.

.FRACTIONAL BANKING

This is actually referred to as fractional "reserve" banking. Lenders are allowed to loan a maximum of up to 20 to one. This is perfectly legal, practiced by every lending institution in America and elsewhere.

Example: Mr. A goes to his friendly banker, Mr. B, and deposits one thousand dollars ($1,000) into Mr. B's bank. Mr. B's bank is a Savings and Loan so Mr. A puts the $1,000 into his own savings account. The Savings and Loan is required by your laws, to keep only 5% in reserve. They are allowed to loan out 95% of the money invested or 95% of that which is placed into savings accounts. This means of $1,000 there is $950 which is available to be loaned out. In turn the Savings and Loan takes the $950 and loans it to Mr. C to do some home repairs, let us say. This gentleman takes his borrowed $950 and goes to the local hardware/lumber company and purchases supplies, lumber, nails etc.

The lumber company carries on regular banking and therefore, he goes to his bank with the $950 for deposit, to Bank D. Bank D is now required to keep 5% but can loan out 95% which would be $902.50. Bank D now loans that to Mr. X who in turn filters it back into the economy, let us suppose, through the grocery store and other business stores. He spends it and now we are going to have that money end up in the Bank Z. Bank Z is required to keep 5%. That means that Bank Z can loan out $857.37. It is again loaned and filterd back into the economy. This is continued right down to zero. With your $1,000 deposit those bankers using fractional reserve banking are now allowed to loan out $20,229.60. This is practiced by EVERY lending institution in

America and elsewhere. The amounts above do not include "interest" on the money borrowed, only the principal amount.

You must now keep it in mind that this results in an increase in the money supply through the Federal Reserve System. Your "big boys" simply turn up the speed of your money presses and run them a little faster and faster in order to pump more into the economy just to boost up the fractional reserve banking. Let me remind you to keep in mind that the thirteen families control all of the hard currencies of the world and are allowed to practice this fractional reserve banking -- this will be important as we move along.

THE OIL CRISIS

We will now talk about something referred to, on your planet, as "System 2000", which is a Global Creditors Unilateral plan. This plan went into effect somewhere about the early 1970s. At that time a pentagon official and several other officials visited Nigeria. They went to the Prime Minister and they paid him fifty million dollars ($50 million) to raise the price of his oil to more than double. Nigerian oil is "light crude" of quality such as it is almost pure enough to burn immediately, without distillation, in automobiles. This type of oil sets the price of oil for the entire world. The $50 million was cash across the board with no repayment requirements if Nigeria would double the price of light crude.

We will refer to this as light oil. There are only two locations in the world that have this light oil and, of course, it is the most valuable oil in your world, therefore, it is the standard against which all other oil in the world is measured. So, whoever controlled the price of the light oil at that time controlled the price of all of the oil in the world.

At this point, let us bring the Arabs into this scenario. This will also bring in the Trilateral Commission -- that also includes Mr. Bush. It was now time to bring pressure and persuasion to OPEC. What most of you Americans do not remember is that the United States of America IS A MEMBER OF OPEC. It is kept most low profile.

At that time a "deal was cut" with the Middle Eastern Oil Producers and this is how it went; all buyers were prepared to pay significantly higher prices for the oil--PROVIDED--all Middle Eastern nations supported the United States of America, BY INVESTING THE REVENUES INTO THE BIG BANKS IN AMERICA.

To make this picture clear, you must remember that the Arabs, who are wealthy sheiks today, had been wandering around on camelback in a very big desert. They were nomads and they were certainly most unsophisticated in business affairs. Years earlier when the international bankers found out there was oil in their countries, they went forth and persuaded the Arabs to allow them to produce the oil by financing the oil fields, drilling, rigging -- all supplies including expertise.

After the bankers financed the oil fields they then charged the Arabs usury fees for building the oil supply systems---along with refineries. The usury was quickly repaid because the Arabs became very rich, very quickly. (Way back then you were only paying about 30 cents per gallon in your gasoline stations). Let us now take it further, you go to Nigeria and pay them to double the price of light crude. Unbeknownst to the Arabs, those ones who had become wealthy overnight and didn't know zero about business, much less international finance; the camel nomads; you call them together and say, "We will take the price of crude just as high as you want it to go--IF--you will deposit an established portion of the funds that you get from this NEW PROFIT RISE IN 30 YEAR TIME CERTIFICATES IN CERTAIN MAJOR U.S. BANKS.

Perhaps you ones can now understand the problems you experienced in your early 1970s. Remember the gas lines and the prices of oil skyrocketing? It was because the international bankers, who hold the purses of the world, knew that the increase in the price of oil that was going to the Arabs would come rushing right back to their bank in 30 year time certificates of deposit.

Turn now to the 30 year time deposits and let us examine the banker's plans. Back in the late 70's and early 80's Sheik Ymani and his bunch had no idea that there was a connection between those banks, or that they were the same people that had the controlling interest of the major oil companies. Do you see what has been woven here? After all, how could the camel riding nomads realize the international bankers were "having them" hook, line and up to the fishing pole? How could they possibly know that what was happening through these oil companies, was that the monies were being cycled right back into the selected, no exceptions, banking system? They couldn't and they didn't!

THE CONTROLLING TRUST

Going a long ways back now; in the 1870's the Rockefellers set up something called a Joint Stock Trust. Here I will add, this was just a brief period of time before the American Government declared these trusts illegal. BUT, YOU SEE, THESE ONES COULD FUNCTION FOREVER UNDER WHAT YOU CALL A "GRANDFATHER" CLAUSE. THAT, BROTHERS, IS THE ULTIMATE CONTROLLING FACTOR IN AMERICA OF THE PRIME BANKS AND THE FEDERAL RESERVE BOARD. That "trust" is in the control of the Rockefeller Foundation, and, in turn controls the Federal Reserve Bank and is the method whereby the Internationalists are able to gain control of the currency of the U.S.A.

Does it begin to become reasonable that those New York banks are showing all time record earnings? Yet, all around the rest of your country of the U.S., banks and Savings and Loans are going broke and failing. THAT, FRIENDS, MEANS YOU ARE BEING MANIPULATED RIGHT ALONG WITH THE ARABS AND EQUALLY AS BLINDLY -- WITH NO RECOURSE.

Let us come back now, and speak of the deal which "was cut" (your ones in power love that term) with the Saudi Arabians and ones of the Middle East. These ones were required to put their money into the prime banks; keep in mind that they did not know that the prime banks were able to lend in amounts of twenty to one. (20 to 1 was quite a while ago, it is higher at present). All they were receiving was the interest on the money they had deposited. Worse for them, in some of these countries it is unacceptable to receive interest for religious reasons so they might wait thirty years to get any money from their certificates of deposit. In other words, they did not know that this fractional type of banking could be done, but through this, the bankers of the world were able to gain control of the money of the Arab world, and in turn, the Arab world only received back part of the interest from the money that they placed into the International Banking System----UNDER THESE 30 YEAR TIME DEPOSIT CERTIFICATES.

Through the money gained from the Arabs through the manipulation of the price of oil, and taking the price of gasoline from, let us say, 30 cents a gallon to $1.25 a gallon---there is a lot of money being made. Now, with that money returning into the international banks at 20 to 1, I think you can see the staggering profits. Let us face facts, friends, that money originally came from YOU. Because the bankers had locked in the deposits they were then, in turn, able to make loans to third world nations.

ENTER THIRD WORLD NATIONS

Think back fifteen or twenty years ago when the International Bankers started investing in third world country loans. <u>Look very closely at the countries which are going bankrupt (completely broke) today. It was fully intended that those countries go broke and I will explain that in a little bit.</u>

You might wonder how I know so much. Well, I have the best computer system in the universe and all I have to do is key it up and it is spread out before me. My computers rarely reflect errors; only changes in "probabilities" and perturbations in human action and reactions.

I am sorry, friends, your friendly bankers set it up deliberately so that the third world countries would go broke. You have to pay attention to history and look back to the time when those third world countries were beginning to gain independence and setting up independent governments. It was at such times that these bankers loaned the upstarts great sums of money which actually had come to them through the Arabs, basically.

The international bankers not only wanted, but insured, that these borrowing countries would misuse the fundings. It was fully intended that those countries would go broke. It was prearranged that the funds could be mismanaged through greed and simply be squandered. You must remember that the leaders of these countries had never governed anything or anybody. They knew nothing about government. They had been colonies under the governorship of other larger countries.

The international bankers knew that the leaders were bound to squander the funds. It was known they would have no way to know what to do with them (and they were massive) and so the cycle goes. They were actually squandering money taken from you through the Arabs through high oil prices, etc. Let us now follow it on through.

PUNISHING TEXAS

I will hereby digress to a story from Dharma's earth home state--Texas--most of you have heard of it. Let us go back some years (not too many) to jog some memories. Do you remember someone named John Connelly, who was governor of Texas? Do you recall that he was also in the vehicle and was injured during John Kennedy's assassination? Well, Mr. Connelly was also Under Secretary of the Treasury--he was a lot of things and titles. These ones with Mr. Connelly did a most fascinating thing--they planned to implement a new currency for the State of Texas. You see, Texas is a part of the Union only through a renewable "treaty". The treaty is automatically renewed every year, but it isn't necessary that it be renewed. That means, friends, that the U.S. only has a treaty with Texas to keep it in the union of states. It was not voted in as were your other states.

Texas was at one time -- I believe your term might be "filthy rich". The state was wealthy and there were many very, very wealthy individuals. Rich individuals such as the Hunt brothers, who actually had nothing originally, but became extremely wealthy, overnight, by OIL. That was all the way back when oil was first struck and became so very popular.

I am truly going to tie all this together but you must bear with me for there are so many facets. I must make it clear what I am going to say. I will explain to you why, if you don't already know, it was so very important to ones of "the opposition", and why there was an assassination attempt against Mr. Connelly's life as well as Kennedy's.

Why are those men "broken" today and a state in severe financial trouble? It is because the Internationalist's learned of what the Hunt brothers and Mr. Connelly were trying to do. Texas, a state by treaty, can legally secede from your union. The Hunt brothers and Mr. Connelly knew that Texas had the ability to set up their own country and have their own currency. That is why they could be solvent and not be under the dictates of the Federal Reserve System. Or, simply stated, under the control of the international bankers.

At about the same time they were in the process of gaining a corner on the silver of the world. This was in order to finance a process whereby they could overcome the international bankers and it was at that point the Hunt brothers were smashed. John Connelly was almost killed, and Texas, which could have been the only state in the union to fulfill breaking out of the trap, has been punished with some extremely major problems. Today, portions of Dallas and Fort Worth, Houston and other wealthy, wealthy cities have gone on to resemble ghost towns in your Old West. Ones who had grown rich in the oil industry have been severely punished, the Hunts and Connelly are bankrupt.

The Internationalists became so incensed, so angry, at what these Texan's had done that they broke the back of the oil industry, and the major oil producers of Texas. It was a well designed plan and executed in perfection.

When ones attempt to interfere with the plans of the international bankers, you can see what the results can be. The Hunt brothers were working directly with the Shah of Iran, on the above plan. Immediately thereafter one of the Texas bankers was killed, the Shah of Iran was deposed, and the Hunt brothers were forced into bankruptcy.

There are many ways the international bankers can get revenge on ones who attempt interference with their overall plan; through murder, or you might well be placed into a mental institution and locked away permanently, or you can have trumped up charges brought against you whereby you are locked away indefinitely in prison. This latter has also happened to numerous ones in the "UFO" investigation circles who find and bring forth truth. It is exactly what happened to Colonel Wendelle Stevens. Colonel Stevens probably has investigated more UFO incidents than any other one individual. Further, an assassination plot was arranged and attempted while Colonel Stevens was incarcerated. Strangely, the perpetrator, who dressed as a religious leader, was caught in the act, turned over to the FBI, and has never been heard from again. So be it.

THE SHAH'S DEATH

If you will recall, the Shah of Iran was in perfect health when he was deposed and departed Iran. He was only declared to be sick after he reached the United States. You were told he was being held in "protective" custody at a military base. There, you were also told, he was being treated for his illness----which was not present at the time of his arrival. He died anyway, didn't he? Face it---his death was planned and the murder executed.

In your present months there is an international uproar over the use of chemical and germ warfare utilized Iran and Iraq. Some of the viruses cannot be traced -- nor, in such above instances, would anyone dare to pursue it.

Who would question a man becoming ill, being treated and then expiring unexpectedly? Certainly no one in the United States would question it. It was uncomfortable enough just having the man in your country. Death can most effectively be brought about in any number of non-traceable ways; one of which is through micro-dots and variations of vibration frequencies, as well as through viruses. (This is exactly what happened to Dharma, in her own dwelling--causing cardiac arrest. We just happen to have her under constant monitoring for she is a receiver of several of us in this higher frequency dimension; therefore, we can catch these attempts and can counter them. Doesn't do much for the mental relaxation of the victim, however.)

THE HOSTAGE STORY

You can get verification of these little stories from Senator John Hansen of your own government. I am going to speak of Iran and your people who were taken hostage. I doubt many of you have heard the truth of the matter.

Senator Hansen was in the House of Representatives in Washington, D.C. He knew what was happening in Iran and requested permission to go to Iran and investigate. Congress refused. Mr. Hansen then purchased his own private airline ticket and proceeded to Iran anyway.

When Senator Hansen arrived, the one Khomeini proffered an audience. Guess what the Khomeini said? He said, "We don't want these hostages, certainly not any more than you want us to have them". "As a matter of fact," Khomeini continued; "I'd like to give you these hostages, at least half of them anyway, and you can take them home with you tomorrow morning. That is, Mr. Hansen, if you will promise to begin an investigation into the relationship between the Shah of Iran, Chase Manhattan Bank, Mr. Henry Kissinger and your President Carter."

At this point, Senator Hansen was most delighted. He rushed to call back to the U.S. to someone who could give authorization and said, "Hey, I can bring half of the hostages home tomorrow. How shall I arrange it?" The person on the other end of the line said, "Well, I will call you back tomorrow and let you know.". Now please guess what happened on the following morning? When the call was placed back to Mr. Hansen, he was told the following, "Get yourself on the next airplane coming to America. Come home immediately. Do not bring hostages. Do not do any negotiating. You have no right to speak on the part of the Congress of the United States of America even if you are a congressman. Get home immediately with no further discourse."

Here is what he found upon his return to Washington--that the incident was entered into the Congressional record. Further he found that President Carter knew the hostages were going to be taken and further--knew that they were there for a reason and he was not to interfere. Now, you ones get yourself ready for a bomb if you have not already had access to this expose'. The release of the hostages in Iran was negotiated by a negotiator of Chase Manhattan Bank in New York, U.S.A. All outside overt and covert attempts to gain release was a facade. Ask any marine who was involved in the military efforts thereof.

Is it really any wonder to you ones that Iran is all ticked off at you today? Those hostages, and America, were held in terror while bankers got the Shah's money safely into their banks before the Shah was killed and then, in turn, got much of the money belonging to Iran. A pretty wicked way to get Iran's money into the Chase Manhattan Bank so it could remain solvent and be one of the wealthiest institutions in the entire world.

SLEIGHT OF HAND

The international banks formed bank "holding companies" so that they could not be held responsible. The Chase Manhattan, Chemical Bank and J.P. Morgan's bank were the predominant banks for money deposited by the Arabs. The holding companies were formed in order to loan out money to the third world countries while knowing full well that the third world countries were going to go broke.

After the Shah had been destroyed and the money was safely in the banks, there were massive amounts of money loaned to third world countries. These notes were shifted from the banks to the bank holding companies in anticipation of the eventual bankruptcy of the borrowing countries.

One holding company was for the purpose of loaning money to the third world countries. The purpose of the second holding company was to borrow money from the international bank in order to purchase agricultural lands. That means your farms and also certain corporations in the United States. The farms and businesses will probably continue to make some money, but the third world countries are designated to go down. This is ongoing, dear ones, not a passing fancy.

Here things began to happen rapidly and with sleight of hand. There have followed myriads of liquidations, foreclosures and bankruptcies which were effected by the FDIC and FSLIC which are under the total control of the Federal Reserve Board. Literally dozens of banks all over America quickly were, and are, being bought up. But the big question is by whom? Who has the money in sufficient amounts to make such purchases? Further, where could such sums of money originate? The great sums come from the higher oil price money that goes to the Arabs, then deposited into the international bankers' banks. The banks being purchased are then intentionally closed. Some of those banks are still solvent. They are also buying up farm land throughout America through the farmers who are now being put into bankruptcy because of the high American dollar (in relationship to foreign currency). At least this is the way it was up to a year or so ago---it is fluctuating somewhat at the present time for other heinous things are under way which are the next step in the plan. I shall not go into those things in this document for I intend to do a document relative to your economies. First, let us consider what is happening now and has been, for your past few years----a lot of things are being done now through the Oriental communities. Ah so?

WATCH THE HANDS

We are going to now consider currency on a world basis. We will also point out why some of the monetary plans and money making formats are valid and viable.

Let us speak a bit about Mr. Marcos who was recently deposed from the Philippines. This is most typical, friends, so watch the hands closely. A representative of the international bankers' bank went to those ones and said, "Mr. Marcos, we will note all your loans and offer you alternatives. We will forgive all of your loans. You cannot pay them back, you cannot pay back the interest, you can't pay back the principle, but, we would like to make you a bargain. We will just forgive the loans."

Digress time: remember, who did that money belong to that they loaned out to these third world places? It was not the bankers'. Well, of course, it was that Arab money, because of the higher prices that the people all over the world had paid. So, back to what the bankers' say, "We'll just forgive your loans, the principal and the interest and you never have to pay it back --IF (ALWAYS THE IF!)---. The "if" goes about as follows: You have to do away with your national currency, whatever it is. The dollar will be your currency basis of value. You will be set up with a type of debit card system instead of the usual currency system. Then, too, you must give us perpetual rights to all of the natural resources in your country.

Interestingly enough, it was right after that little gift gesture; that friendly little suggestion, that Mr. Marcos was deposed. Why do you suppose that happened? Well, Mr. Marcos was pretty fiesty and he told the international bankers where they could go right after they got immediately out of his country. He had no intention of giving them sovereignty over his country and look what happened.

Everyone in that country found that suddenly their social security number was synonymous with their credit number; further, their central bank was to act as a wholesaler for credit, which in turn, was extended to it by the new super bank which was announced by your Mr. Paul Volker in the fall of 1985. That was ratified immediately by President Reagan. Just a fun aside for you who love to play with numbers and speculate about coincidence---the names and numbers, the digits, added up to six. Lots of things around Mr. Reagan add up to sixes--even his retirement home address. I take very little stock in these things, but many of you seem to like the game. Also, because a President is not reelected does not mean he is vanquished from the fray.

A further contingent condition of the benevolent gift, if you will, of the International Monetary Fund, was that in order to help the economy of those countries the IMF was going to nominate external, nondomestic corporations to properly engineer, exploit and excavate the minerals of those said countries who had just put those same mineral resources up as collateral. This would all, thereby, supposedly bring prosperity to those striving nations.

Mr. Marcos was a bit sharper up front, however, and he pinpointed on the word PERPETUAL in the contract. He realized that quite obviously he would be signing away the sovereignty of his nation.

I make no comment or judgment regarding Mr. Marcos as a person, nor do I make comment about any individual --- those ones are of human format, not mine. I am just telling you the way it is and how some things happened.

In the case of the Marcoses, it was only a matter of weeks before the banker's brought down the guillotine blade. Riots were financed by, and originated through, ones of the international banker's groups. It is never humanly wise to cross these ones;

you see, Mr. and Mrs. Marcos were exploiting the people well enough on their own and did not wish to share.

WHERE DID THE MONEY GO?

Ah, let us not forget those holding companies of which I spoke. Remember holding companies one and holding companies two? The second group was receiving credit from the first group of holding companies to purchase assets and liabilities from the "prime" banks. The only liabilities they would purchase were liabilities represented by Certificates of Deposits of the Arab nations. The assets they were buying were loans made to the debtor nations. Remember, it was designed that third world countries would default on the loans which would bankrupt the holding companies which had purchased the Arab's CD's from the banks.

At such a point, the international bankers say to the Arabs, "OK fellows, sorry, but all those billions of dollars in 30 year term deposits that you have been depositing all these years are gone. They were sold to a holding company, unattached to us, which loaned the money to third world countries which are bankrupt - broke - gone kaput. Sorry Mr. Arab, but as of today you are bankrupt. Just like that--all gone!"

You might ask, "Is it possible for the Arab world to go bankrupt? Really now, the richest people in the world with all that oil?" It is a little bit shocking isn't it? Poor souls, they didn't even know those CD's had been "sold" to those holding companies. They had deposited the money right into the New York bank as required. How could they possibly know they were transferred out and into bankruptcy destined companies? How could they understand the inner manipulations of international financiers? They were nomads, they didn't know anything about business. One cannot even consider them foolish. How much of this intrigue do you know, much less understand?

The Arabs could not know what they were up against. But now let us look at what has happened. Before the end of 1986 the Arab world became a bit aware of what was happening to them. The word went out that before May 1st, 1987 millions and millions had to be transferred out of the Arab world into America, to start preparing for doomsday. Money was to be shifted into any kind of securities that were even half way decent. Why do you think this was so? It was so that when the Arab sheiks came to the point of bankruptcy they could be sure the people under them, those millions of people of the Arab countries who have literally been "kept" by give-away programs, could not get at them. They would have a place to run to and, hopefully, hide. Well, when this all comes down that these Arab countries have literally been sold out, innocently or knowingly, there will be uprisings, turmoil and literally, massacres abounding. It is going to happen, friends, right in the Arab nations.

This is why they have purchased, and set in place, silkworm type missiles from China. Long range, nuclear capable, and they have the nuclear devices to arm them. Could it be they will be needed against their own peoples? The people are going to be quite irritated when they are no longer receiving anything from the oil revenues, that their own country is bankrupt and that further, they were sold out by their own leaders. At that point there will be mass migration of sheiks headed for America where they have already transferred the most of their assets.

The Arabs were trying to make the big purchases by May of 1988; it is now a year and a half later. Do you not think things might be starting to come down pretty soon? Could it be relatively correlated in timing to Savings and Loan problems and private pension plan troubles and failing economy and - and -?

I continue to see problems as I look upon my scanners. The probability of you making it into your 1990 before a major depression is not reflected there. I see no way for you to make it past your fall season.

You only need a couple more countries to default and your monetary system will collapse. You sit on the target for several methods of pulling you down into collapse. Well, back to the original story.

We are talking of holding companies in trouble. The international bankers have removed responsibility from themselves. They passed the notes, etc. on to the holding companies who in turn made the bad loans. All that money belonging to the Arabs has been passed on into the holding companies. All the international bankers have to do is say to the Arabs, "You are broke. As of today--all gone!" When the Arabs demand payment of the 30 year term notes, the holding companies are insolvent - simple as that, no funds--broke.

Do you see now, that this group "made" people some years back and now they can "break" them with equal speed and efficiency without being accountable?

I fear, friends, it is not very different from what is being done unto you dear ones. * * * * * * * but, that is another story.

WHAT HAPPENS NEXT?

What happens next after this point in insolvency and negotiations, is that the assets would have to be liquidated. The Arabs now have to liquidate. They bought farm land, for instance, all over America. Likewise they bought stocks in a lot of corporations as well as a lot of bonds and some other kinds of real estate. In fact, they have controlled a large portion of the New York Stock Exchange. Keep in mind the Japanese control a large portion, also.

Let us look at the morning following the notice of bankruptcy. The Arabs will dump their stocks onto the New York Stock Exchange and what is going to happen when billions of dollars worth of their stock comes on the market? I am talking billions and billions of dollars and, suddenly, there it all is to be sold!

What happens to farm land that is already depressed? In 1987 prime farmland that had been worth $3,000 an acre was less than $700 per acre because of deflation and the inability to repay farm loans. Now you have added drought and all sorts of other bad dreams. By the way, this deflation was brought about by your Federal Reserve System. Well, the Arabs don't want that farmland, they have all the problems they can handle. What happens to the price of the farmland? It is going right to the floor isn't it? Brothers, when that happens with the value what does it mean? It means it has no collateral value any longer. With no collateral value, how can a farmer borrow money next year for his crops? In turn, what happens to the crops? Who is going to feed the people? What is going to happen in the grocery markets? The results, of course, equates to hunger and scarce supply. Sad, brothers, but it is a well laid out plan working to perfection.

It all boils down to CONTROL and how do you ever recover. Further, let us look at your stock situation. What is going to happen when these multitudes of stocks are dumped on the stock market? Chaos. What will be the result of catastrophic chaos? IT HAS BEEN DESIGNED TO THROW THE AMERICAN STOCK EXCHANGES, PRIVATE CORPORATIONS, PRIVATE BUSINESS, AMERICAN REAL ESTATE AND QUITE FRANKLY, THE PEOPLE IN GENERAL, INTO A STATE OF TOTAL CONFUSION.

TO THE RESCUE!

Let me finish the plan for you. At the time of total confusion and inability to function, those benevolent bankers are going to come through with a "save the world proposal". They are going to be prepared to eliminate cash because of its collapse. Secondarily, they must then stop drug trafficking. Then, they must also push to stop tax cheating. Now, what self respecting American citizen can possibly be against such noble efforts? They (the bankers) have set up and orchestrated all of these programs and now will pretend to stop them.

What will the average American do when your television says, "Look at what those dirty Arabs have done to you?" What would you do? You are going to believe what they tell you, aren't you? You are going to be right up there in front saying, "Sure they did it to us. Those Arabs want to control the world." Pretty soon it will be, "Those Japanese want to control the whole world," and then, "The Chinese want to control the whole world." You will join the chant that says, "Look, they bought up all of this major part of America. Look at all the money we have given them, and see what they have done. They have collapsed our stock market , et cetera and so on". Ah ha, but here come your benevolent bankers and they are going to say to you, "You have got to have a new currency and then the next thing we will do is use that new currency to stop this dope trafficking. You know, that which is coming in from Central America and those other countries. Then, of course, we are also going to have to have a debit card to stop people from tax cheating because, after all, Mr. Public, if we don't do this we will never get ourselves back on our feet. ---So, brothers, if you'll just turn everything over to us benevolent bankers we will take care of everything and straighten out the whole mess." You know what, brethren? You will hop on that bandwagon and agree to your imprisonment like babes to candy. You will not only agree to it; you will demand it. For you will forget to hear the big IF. "YOU WILL GET ALL THIS DONE FOR YOU **IF** YOU WILL JUST TAKE A DEBIT CARD FOR YOU INDIVIDUALLY WITH OUR LITTLE OLD NUMBER ON IT!" YOU WILL HAVE JUST FALLEN FOR THE OLD IDENTIFICATION CARD SCHEME.

HOW CAN THIS HAPPEN TO YOU? BECAUSE YOU HAVE NEVER BEEN TOLD THE TRUTH, FRIENDS, AND WILL YOU BELIEVE IT NOW AS I GIVE IT TO YOU? NO, MOST OF YOU WILL DISCOUNT ME AS A FIGMENT OF SOME NUT'S WILD IMAGINATION. SO BE IT FOR I AM GREATLY SADDENED FOR YOU AS A SPECIES.

THE NEW CURRENCY

This has been a scenario about the Middle East. Where do you think you are today and what do you think you will be when you have this new currency? It will only devaluate the old "dollar" to zero. It is planned already and named already; the Phoenix. A little prior to this, there is a plan to bring forth an international credit card ID. Let us refer to it as a government ID card with your social security number on it which would be, and get this because the next is important, satellite linked through the Star Wars system. Does any of this sound familiar to you? This program of Star Wars is at least 60% geared towards this very purpose and only 40% for the claimed defense systems, etc.

This major space linkup will facilitate the transmission of banking information throughout the world instantly. This would be a debit card with a number which would be required for you to do business, and friends, if you know anything at all about your Biblical prophecies, God has already told you it will be, it will take place. Further, it will be done in such a clever way that you "Christians" who say you will NEVER sign up nor participate will never see it hit you and you will have joined the program without even realizing it. How else are you going to survive? Let us not be foolish in our claims for you are dealing with most clever planners who have out thought you completely up to this date.

Now, I hope you will believe me when I tell you that the "Star Wars" program of satellite systems is in place. Satellites are up there, friends. We of other planets are allowed to stop nuclear warheads---we are not permitted to touch satellites which are not geared to some type of nuclear detonation.

Well, all those wonder filled bits of technology called eyes in the sky and spy satellites "for your security" are really for the purpose of transfer of the very banking and income information which I have just been describing. It can set up immediate transfer of funds from all over the entire world, from the debit card, that the internationalists will see to it are established with every living person. You will be on the system whether you know it or not. In fact, you who are old enough to read these words ---- and every child ---- is already entered therein.

All information will be entered into a central computer and from that place the world will come under instant financial control. So, dear Americans, you have just paid your hard earned money to finance that program to initiate the bankers' international credit card system and number system that will be implemented whether or not you choose of it. IT IS DONE, BROTHERS, IT IS IN PLACE---DONE! DON'T TELL ME YOU WILL NOT PARTICIPATE---YOU ARE ALREADY A PARTICIPANT, DEAR LITTLE ONES.

Oh yes, what of your defense system? Doesn't look too good does it? Well, we are not going to let those nuclear warheads out here in our space past one hundred fifty miles anyway. That is our prerogative and we stop them or dismantle them.

HEAR ME

Do you not see, brothers, that this is the way the prophecies are coming into your focus? It is happening all about you but you don't seem to know what it is you look for.

Please, all I want you to do at present is HEAR ME. There is naught you can do about it to any great extent as it stands.

You who will hear me and mine own groups, hear me. You must utilize all of the remaining time to its maximum efficiency for we will have to continue to work under the new systems. Our projects will never be less than excellent investments and they must, and will, be funded. It needs to be done rapidly, however, before we are caught up in total collapse of the monetary system. We can work through depression if we have fundings--monetary collapse shuts us down for all practical purposes, until the system can be put on track and functioning.

It can work and will work, for in these confused, rushed and harassed days there is great madness to shift money and make money on money and etc. Countries such as China, Japan --- all non hard currency countries are desperate to convert to dollars.

I will further tell you that your governments know we are here. They also know we are not here to interfere. We are here to walk our people through a transition and we plan nothing subversive. We do plan good business ventures and welcome all who wish to participate. We have no communes, all work for fair reward. We plan good business with total integrity and latest technology. We are here to help, not overthrow. We are here only to walk our brothers through, for it will all come down just as the prophecies are given. There will be some very bad times ahead most surely if plans are not made for those days of tribulation.

Let me speak a bit more regarding "timing". I know that what I have said is truth.

It was confirmed by top sources in Switzerland that by October of last year there were twelve debtor nations who had agreed to the proposal of debt forgiveness in exchange for perpetual consignment of natural resources. There only need to be one or two more that give enough leverage to announce the Arabs bankrupt. As of now, all the top leaders in the Arab world know the story and they are scared to death about it. They don't know what they are going to do about it; there is actually nothing they can do about it. They certainly do not know how to announce it to their populace. There doesn't seem to be any way to get the information out to the people.

Further, no one knows how to announce all this to the American people. It has been attempted by some and fallen on deaf ears. I hope that by the time many of you have read this document, there will be recognition of our presence in your space. What I tell you is truth.

IN SUMMARY

I would like now, to sum up this scenario.

Because the 20 to 1 debt to asset banking ratio also operates in reverse (that's how it is with leverage), it only takes about five percent of the third world countries to declare bankruptcy and when they do, and they accept the plan of the international bankers, then the bankers can declare the bank holding companies bankrupt. Because of the reverse leverage of the loans, only 5% of the third world countries could basically declare the world bankrupt and the ownership of all falls to the international bankers.

When this program is initiated and in place, it will wind up with the international bankers owning all mortgages and all properties. What is that going to do to your country? What about the world? What control will they have when they initiate the debit card? It will be an automatic number which will be given and would be required because the country is devastated.

It would then result that the international bankers, who are made up of all these secret and complex committees I have previously discussed, would now own the majority of the United States and most other countries (for all will fall in short order), would control the Arab world and therefore, by about a thirty year plan of manipulation, will have brought the peoples of the world under control.

Two years ago, your Senator George Hansen said you had only about a year to get this under control, to get the information out and do something about it. Well, your year has passed into two and a half. How much have you heard about it? I doubt very much. Brothers, this is how men make slaves of their fellow men.

It has, however, been prophesied since the beginning of your world that these things would come to pass. This statement is not to give you negative feelings. This is to tell you that you are IN the time of the evolution of your planet where these things are now coming to be.

I go through all this that you might recognize the signs which are all around you. The time, in your perception of time, is fleeting. The "time" we call sequence of events -- is fleeting. We have much to do and we are here and available to assist you ones of God and the children of your planet called Earth Terra. You are a sister planet to we of Pleiades. Many of our ones walk among you. There are many duties and jobs that must now be finished.

The story, the work, will go out for that is God's promise to man. His promise is to allow man to hear and to see, followed by proof. He will send these things through us of the space brotherhood.

These things shall be documented and sent forth to man so that man can see what he wishes to do---what choices he wishes to make regarding his divinity.

I am going to leave this portion now, that you ones can ponder these things.

We come in love and we can see farther than you. We have access to all records, so we can see and know. We can give assistance if we are so petitioned. And you might ask, "Why would you ones do that?" Because Father God the Totality, the Light which is your Source and My Source loved you enough to send forth His Celestial Son, before us. We now serve that same "Son" who is our Commander and act in His service.

Further, for you who are our brothers, we will not leave you stranded on that place. Ye who do not yet know me, will come to understanding of our presence. I leave mine seal and my blessings on this portion, which I fear is quite lengthy. Please ponder it several times until you have understanding for it is most important.

Go Dharma, it has been such a terribly long session for you. Turn the papers over to the others that you may get some rest.

Salu, Salu, Salu   Hatonn moving to stand-by.

CHAPTER 3

REC #1, HATONN

WEDNESDAY, AUGUST 30, 1989 6:30 A.M. YEAR 3, DAY 014

LET US MOVE SMARTLY ALONG PLEASE.

RECESSION OFF?

Yesterday on your news(?) programs it was touted on every station. "GNP is up one and a half points from the month before---recession is off!" Day before yesterday: "Stock market hit all time high!---recession off!" Then yesterday, "Stock market fell BUT it was due to profit takers from yesterday's all time high.---recession off!" YOUR RECESSION IS NOT 'OFF'! YOUR DEPRESSION IS VERY MUCH 'ON'! YOU HAVE NOTHING UPON WHICH TO BASE YOUR PICTURED PAPER FLOW. THE SYSTEM IS QUITE DEAD, JUST AS ARE THE ONES PICTURED ON YOUR PAPERS.

Dharma, I realize you know naught of finance nor international economics. I care not, chela. Please, I will make an effort to not move so rapidly. I do not, however, want you to even "think" about it as we move along here for it only slows us; you can come into understanding elsetime.

These messages and suggestions are put forth for my people who are asking for assistance in order to maintain working ability for we are building a new business structure. The only way you can do so, and survive at the same time, is to use clever strategy. Because my vision is farther out front than is yours, I can assist. I can also see "the trees within the forest".

Let me give you some figures. They are obsolete, of course, but you need a full year, in your counting, to form a picture. To save time, which is the only way you are going to gain value from this dissertation, is to utilize some of your own published figures lest you spend all your time checking on the reality of one Hatonn. I am going to quote a lot of things, selectively, so that I might give you reasoning to take action.

WHAT IS MONEY?

Firstly, what is money? The paper money you spend has as collateral a U.S. Government Treasury Bond. Remember that, it is not gold, my friends. Therefore, government credit is money. So, if the government's credit is not good, neither is the money you spend. Further, neither is the value of mortgages, CD's, mutual funds, and any other "paper", since they are all measured in "dollars". In a very short time the dollar will be worthless. It's very much a form of suicide---intent and fulfillment.

Do you realize that approximately four banks in the U.S. fail in each of your weeks? This does not count the ones being absorbed by the gray man banking octopus (relative to the gray men lecture). I state, "failing". This is because they are in the state of petrification. Only a very small portion of most banks' assets can be liquidated on short notice without very large losses.

Commercial banks rely on the Federal Reserve to replenish their reserves--DAILY--good weather or bad. But guess what---the Federal Reserve Banks are not in much better shape: they consist of government securities. In case of a bank run, the Federal Reserve would be in no position to meet the demand for cash -- remember the minimum 20 to one lending ratio? If a demand for cash through honest liquidation were allowed, it would absolutely break the bond market. Therefore, the Federal Reserve System (FED) would have to do what it has already begun to do---monetize by CREATING CREDITS--- not PAPER MONEY; the bad assets of the banks needing aid only makes the FED's own position incredibly worse. Therein lies great and magnificent danger, friends.

Most of you, the U.S. public, and, frankly, most of your experts live in a dreamworld. You peer into your personal computers (experts) and the television screens (public) and eat up the projections of paid projectionists who tell you exactly that which is fed to them. Most of you believe you are still a nation that you have been in the past times---one that furiously produces goods and services so that everyone can have a wondrously high standard of living. You believe that it is your capitalistic system and its profit drive that makes it all possible. (News flash: you haven't had a true capitalistic system in such a long, long time.) You believe that you work for money, money is your main goal, and you get this money by hard work. WRONG!

GOODS OR MONEY?

Since the turn of your last century America has been transformed from a system of making goods to one of making money; that is, there is more money to be made by playing with and juggling money than by working to make goods. Proof? Always you want proof! Let us go back to ancient times when the figures were inclusive, let us say 1986. There was $2 trillion in goods traded internationally and $36 trillion in capital transfers.

Dharma cannot even spell the numbers of trillions transferred in ONE DAY presently.

It was, in the ancient past, that banks made money making small loans to the public. Now they rake in leviathan fees for lending in LEVERAGED BUY OUT deals. They will lend to a merger deal for a very large fee; i.e.: "Banks made $380 million on the Nabisco deal alone, and they will make close to $300 million in the Time-Warner debt-merger-insanity.

This appears crazy, does it not? After all, all of this debt--these loans they are making--are going to have to be repaid some day, aren't they? If not, then Time-Warner goes down a deep hole and takes its large and very friendly New York City banks with them! So be it---remember my lectures? Exactly what is intended, public, exactly what is intended--with both parties knowing truth. All moves right back into the plan and the magnificent banking "own the world" system. They will never be repaid---just as third world country debt--it is not intended that it ever be repaid. All participants are a part of the Trilateral Commission; Council on Foreign Relations and International Monetary Fund. OH YES, BELOVED ONES, YOU ARE BEING LED DIRECTLY INTO THE DRAGON'S MOUTH AND IT IS PAST THE POINT OF NO RETURN. WE HAVE TRIED TO TELL YOU THIS FOR YEARS BUT, "THERE ARE NO SPACE MEN OR UFO'S".

Let us speak briefly about the "quality" of credit. The sole aim of government spending should be to keep the credit of the government at the highest possible level and above all suspicion. (I don't really have to go further, do I?) That statement means that the government must borrow only if it can see revenues in the years ahead which can be used to retire the debt. If this should happen (and it happened in your ancient historical past), the rate of interest would be stable and quite low. Now, there is NO WAY--NO CHANCE of ever retiring your government debt, therefore, interest rate gyrations prove my point. They move like runaway rockets--crazy, up --- and a bit down --- but never steady. They are manipulated to "assist" the economy--or so you are told so you can be distracted from that which is really going on under the covers.

The quality of all outstanding credit in your America cannot be higher than that of the government, so the ongoing deterioration of the government's credit adversely affects every single one of you.

I suggest you start, right now, looking into survival gear and survival foods. You think I chuckle -- nay, I do, unfortunately, mean it. I will at some point along here give you some preferred places to seek out these resources.

DEBT

I will take the explanation of your debts a bit further (and beloved ones, I do not even yet speak of your personal debts, which comprise the major portion of the overall debt. Remember those credit cards?). I will speak in generalities about national debt in your country.

The domestic debt in America is not without its magnificent danger. It can easily be compared to "nuclear" energy. Controlled and constrained it can be enormously beneficial. Out of control it can be enormously destructive and further, just as with fissionable matter, without any apparent bad effects. Up to a point you appear to be fine---but once critical point is reached--WHAM--MELTDOWN AND CHAIN REACTION BEYOND RECOVERY!

On October 20, 1987, your New York Stock Exchange came within five minutes of closing down. Had that occurred, it would have taken at least five years to gain ability to reopen. And that perturbation was minor compared to what is headed your way when the OIL KINGDOMS DUMP! You do not even have a tightrope upon which to tread--your rope is wound so tightly and so tattered and frayed that it will reach critical point and snap, in the blink of an eye.

What is good debt vs. bad debt, you ask of me? It is not arbitrary--it is judged by its productivity. This is the ratio of net gain in Gross National Product to the gain in debt (the net gain in GNP is the excess of additional GNP over additional debt).

If this ratio is positive, then the new debt can be serviced out of current income. The greater the ratio, the higher the quality of the debt--like consumers having enough income to easily pay what they owe. BUT if the productivity of debt (meaning the income it produces) becomes negative and interest can no longer be paid out of current income, then new debts have to be originated to meet the maturing debt. This negative ratio is a clear sign that bad debt is now breeding and multiplying more bad debt. This feedback short-circuits the economic process.

The debt-tower is then out of control and in due time must self-destruct. THAT IS WHERE YOU ARE, BROTHERS, AT CRITICAL POINT--RIGHT AT CORE MELTDOWN BLAST-OFF! Hold to your seat belts: You have a GNP of around $4 trillion AND DEBT OF ABOUT $12 TRILLION. YOUR DEBT IS **NOT PRODUCTIVE. YOU PRODUCE DEBT, NOT WEALTH!** DEAR ONES, YOU WILL PAY THE PIPER IN THE FORM OF A LONG DEPRESSION. This is the only way to close the gap between your GNP and debt.

You now ask, "Hatonn, then when will it collapse?" IT ALREADY HAS. IF YOUR FED TRIED TO BORROW THE KIND OF REAL MONEY NEEDED, THE FINANCIAL MARKETS WOULD BE IN TOTAL COLLAPSE.

Now I will quote directly from your own statistics: (Credit to Dr. John King, Future Economic Trends, August, 1989.) (Editor's note: the quote is direct; if the numbers do not add properly it is not the error of the Author.) "As of September 30, 1988, the formal debt of the Federal Government was $2.6 trillion, and this excludes their contingent liabilities which, to most Americans, are an accounting curiosity. The government debt maturity, on average, is just 4 1/2 years. In the early 1930's it was 50 years and in 1947, 20 years.

"The Federal Government Contingent Liabilities are as follows: DIRECT GOVERNMENT LOANS: $222 BILLION, GUARANTEES ON LOANS BY U.S.: $550 BILLION, LOANS BY GOVERNMENT AGENCIES: $720 BILLION TOTAL: $1.5 TRILLION!

"To this must be added government deposit insurance guarantees: $1.5 trillion in S&L's, $1.5 trillion in Commercial Banks, and $700 billion in Credit Unions (FSLIC, FDIC, Federal Credit Union Insurance)---a TOTAL OF OVER $3 TRILLION. All government debts total over $8 TRILLION. Uncle Sam is strung out on a debt limb, more than most people can realize.

"The Thrift Crisis (S&L's) has given all of us a taste of how fast these contingent liabilities can turn into real dollar losses. Early on, the Thrift Crisis was estimated at $20 billion, then $150 billion, then $237 billion, and now $400 billion (WALL STREET JOURNAL, Martin Mayer, May 14, 1989). My own guess is that the thrift deposit total is $1 trillion. Why so large? Uncle Sam does not have the resources to save that size debt, and neither do the taxpayers--consumers buried as they are in debt. The coming Credit Meltdown will prove the accuracy of this observation.

CREDIT MELTDOWN

"When will this happen? Actually, it has already started. The 'solution' by Congress of the S&L crisis is another Band Aide. Why don't they do more? A lack of funds--if the FED tried to borrow the kind of real money needed, the financial markets would be wrecked in the process. Not far ahead we will all be witness to that terrible fiasco---meltdown."

Now comes a very formidable situation. When your Treasury gets ready to refinance its debt, it is at the mercy of the financial markets. In fiscal year 1990 (Which by the way, starts October first--ONE MONTH FROM TODAY!), the Treasury will have to refinance $670 billion in debt. That, friends, is on top--above and beyond-- any NEW borrowing.

Short-term rates are on the rise, and this makes refunding more costly. Also, lurking in the distance is the worry that the markets will begin to worry about the "credit worthiness" (you know, your TRW credit report), of your Government, Uncle Sam.

So far the financial markets globally have been remarkably complacent. No one harbors the thought that the U.S. government might go broke --- or do they? The world bankers are "banking" on it! The public truly believes that the government's promise to pay thrift and bank and other bad debts is a fact. BUT, THE GOVERNMENT TELLS YOU THAT GOD IS IN HIS HEAVEN, THEREFORE, ALL IS WELL WITH THE WORLD---WHY WORRY, AND BESIDES, THE WORLD SERIES IS COMING UP WITH OR WITHOUT PETE ROSE.

THE GOVERNMENT HAS JUST VERY ARTFULLY MERGED ONE INSOLVENT BUSINESS INTO ANOTHER AND, AT ALL COSTS, KEPT THE REAL LOSSES FROM HAPPENING TO YOU. PRAY THEY CAN PLAY THAT GAME JUST A BIT LONGER UNTIL I CAN SUGGEST SOME PERSONAL POSSIBILITIES.

Evidence is growing that the government has very little overall capacity to make good on its own debts.

If the S&L (thrift) fiasco is not bad enough, in early June Brian Hyland, Inspector General for the Labor Department, said that more than $1.6 TRILLION in PENSION FUNDS is potentially at risk because of poor regulations and inept enforcement of federal laws. Mr. Hyland added, "These are savings American workers have set aside for their future. These workers trust that the government will protect these funds by holding managers and trustees of their pension funds accountable." (So what, do you know any trustees or managers who have $1.6 trillion?) He continued, "As has been demonstrated by the recent savings and loan crisis, government regulation of an industry does not ensure that invested assets are protected. "The $100 billion Congress estimates the rescue of the thrifts to cost will appear to be a 'bargain'" (Already obsolete isn't it---$200 billion and growing!) "should a similar crisis wrack a significant number of the nation's 870,350 private pension funds. The funds hold $1.6 trillion in assets. The government insuring agency, the Pension Benefit Guarantee Corporation, is itself in financial trouble NOW." Oh my, the Labor Department has worked long into every night to discredit Mr. Hyland just as the government works at discrediting anyone who speaks truth.

THE GUN IS COCKED

All it will take to bring down the house of cards--THE FINANCIAL SYSTEM--is a change in perception of those that buy government debt. If they become truly worried about the Treasury's willingness and ability to honor its debts, the debt game is OVER-DONE-FINIS! AND, BROTHERS, THE JAPANESE HAVE BEEN MOVING MORE AND MORE AWAY FROM SUPPORTING YOUR DEBT AND THEY HAVE BEEN CARRYING YOU FOR A LONG TIME! THEY ARE BUYING LESS AND LESS OF YOUR DEBT WHILE BUYING MORE AND MORE OF YOUR REAL ESTATE TO GET THE LAST BIT OF VALUE FROM YOUR DOLLAR.

Keep in mind, also, that the contingent liabilities above are the items that might cause loss in confidence. These are debts that the government has put its guarantee behind---BUT---are not part of the $2.6 trillion in formal dept.

Note how fast these contingent liabilities can turn into real dollar losses. Look at the Thrift Crisis. Add the potential Pension Crisis. (Worse, by tomorrow you will have additional crises.) A part of the problem is compounding interest, a most ridiculous spiral of disaster.

Currently, you (taxpayers) are servicing the public debt, and it will never be retired. Taxation, given time, can only grow worse--it must. Moreover, the creditworthiness of the government can suddenly vanish if creditors lose faith (or decide against supporting you), in the ability of the government to eventually retire the public debt. Do you also see why you cannot afford to give up the billions of dollars gleaned by the drug intercourse?

A great deal of the annual increase in debt now can be accounted for by the high rate of interest the government must pay. The interest payment is far in excess of the productivity of labor and capital, and it is created out of thin air to keep the game of musical chairs going. But this merry-go-around must stop sooner or later, and when it does, it is CATASTROPHE FOR ALL OF YOU.

THE GRAY NINETIES

Please allow me to list a few things and then we can get down to some hard possibilities for saving your assets. Just a few things your friendly Mr. Bush faces in the "GRAY NINETIES": (Again quoting Dr. King.)

"PEARL HARBOR NO. 2. The Japanese Investor Army has gobbled up the best parts of Hawaii for breakfast. They are now having lunch on California and lunch dessert of Washington D.C. Dinner hour is arriving fast, and this time Mr. Bush won't get a quick rescue!

"NATIONAL DEBT. $2.6 TRILLION AND CLIMBING LIKE A ROCKET. Interest is a miserly 15% of the national budget at present. But, by the end of 1989, it will likely be doubled. How far is it from that point to bankrupt-city?

"TRADE DEFICIT. At $160 billion, this is actually more pressing than the national debt. Your trading partners are really getting miffed off at you.

"CORPORATE DEBT. This is worse than the government debt. It is a million wobbly dominoes on a shaky table--all lined up. Leveraged buy-outs have wreaked havoc on debt.

"PRIVATE DEBT. The credit card mentality is pandemic, and nobody seems to care. Just offer more and more and you take and spend more and more. Over half your country lives from paycheck to paycheck and saves naught. Worse, much of that paycheck goes to paying off "old" purchases and interest. You believe an really upscale lifestyle is now your birthright. Well, you are taking VCRs, computer clones, Suzuki's and Hondas in trade for all that Hawaii and California real estate.

"SAVINGS AND LOANS. The charade is over. Your FDIC is a total mirage and the FSLIC is some $17 billion in the debit hole. both are being kept alive on life support systems in the form of an intravenous continuous drip line running from the Treasury Department. BROTHERS, THE 'QUIET' BANK RUNS HAVE ALREADY BEGUN!

"INFLATION. It is back! In fact, it never went anywhere. Private studies of true inflation (you know, those NOT done by your government), have put it, and keep it, well above 10%.

"THE BUREAUCRACY. Ah yes, the government apparatus has become bloated and incredibly expensive. (Please see SPACE-GATE, THE VEIL REMOVED.) Portions of it are legally IMPERVIOUS to change, like your State Department which tends to crucify your friends and aids your enemies.

"THE HOUSE OF CONGRESS. The ultimate problem is entrenched liberal congressmen. They have taken the richest economy in the world and driven it to its knees. Further, today the reelection rate for those financial morons is 99%!! Now, who votes for the 'PUBLIC SERVANTS'"?

WHAT TO DO FIRST

HOW WOULD YOU SOLVE THESE, AND THE MYRIADS OF ADDITIONAL PROBLEMS SUCH AS THE TRILATERAL COMMISSION, OF WHICH MR. BUSH IS A PRIME PARTICIPANT? WELL, YOU WON'T LIKE THE WAY THE BIG OCTOPUS WILL SOLVE IT, BELOVED FRIENDS, (Again, please refer to SPACE-GATE, THE VEIL REMOVED!) SO BE IT AND PRAY DILIGENTLY!

I can go on and on pointing out all the mess. But you ask, "What do we do?" You take a good confronting look at the truth of it; take off the blinders and really SEE. Then, I am going to make some suggestions for handling your money and your business (from now on they will be inseparable). You must utilize all tools left at your disposal -- before they are appropriated. There are no good solutions. It is much like being in a nuclear war--there is no good place to be---only, perhaps, a place where you might somchow survive until the lifeboat arrives.

The mess is not reversible, it must play itself out--right on through the debit card enslavement for it is too late to do more than try to survive and do as well as you can through it.

You will have a series of expected sequence of events. First you will need to protect your current money assets as much as possible and protect your currently "owned" property. S&L's and Banks will not be a good place to keep anything. Then you will need to get yourself into a tax shelter (the government will appropriate all your funds in the form of taxes until there are no funds left to garner). There is only one shelter that I find on my scanners and that is in incorporation and good corporation management--bunches of small corporations---quite frankly, set up in your State of Nevada. Nevada is the only one of your states within the union that can give you any protection at all.

Dharma, I wish to give you a break, chela, before we continue further.

I TRUST I HAVE GIVEN YOU ENOUGH EXAMPLE THAT YOU WILL AT LEAST LISTEN TO ME. I CAN GIVE YOU A HISTORY OF HOW YOU HAVE CYCLED, RELEASED CONTROL AND HISTORICALLY COME TO THIS POINT--BUT--I PERCEIVE YOU NEED HELP, NOT LECTURES ON HOW, WHY, WHAT, WHEN AND WHERE--YOU ALREADY KNOW WHO! SALU.

CHAPTER 4

REC #2, HATONN

WEDNESDAY, AUGUST 30, 1989 2:00 P.M. YEAR 3, DAY 014

Thank you, Dharma. Hatonn returned to continue.

Let me remind the readers before going further; we are not in the literary business, nor the financial business, nor the corporations business, nor the "book" business. I am here because I have been requested to be here. I am giving input according to the probabilities as they are presented to me. I will tell you what I see; I can do no more. What you do with the information is irrelevant to me or to my scribes. I am here in your space on Higher business and am telling my troops the most effective moves to make RIGHT NOW. You are in a final loop in a tailspin that leaves you very few options.

Your economists can tell you anything they please. You may believe anything you please. You may take the advice or cast it aside. I just suggest that if you cast it aside, you do not come to Hatonn with your moaning and complaints. You ones (your world) are going to go right through the prophetic times according to projections and, right on time. Built in is a very big world wide depression and economic collapse. I'm sorry, but you are also going to undergo a miserable, miserable war.

STRATEGIES, YES---SOLUTIONS, NO

There are no perfect "solutions"; I can only give you what might give you benefit. In other instruction manuals I will try to keep you informed as to the best type of survival facilities and food storage. Yes, there will be hard times ahead but if you heed my words and suggestions you can be a bit prepared. As your brothers from the cosmic realms have the ability to come and go in your behalf, you will be receiving much input and assistance. Many, many have responded to your plea for help--but I promise you this--there will be no abuse nor ridicule of my scribes nor those of Esu Jesus Immanuel Sananda. If you do not know of that which I speak, I suggest you get everything you can from A.S.S.K as we will be giving updated suggestions and instructions through that source--often, regularly and up to the minute.

I suggest you not be too amused at these words. You are in the transition of a world; to and into the final days of the Revelations' prophecies. It will be the ones who come into balance with the Creator God who will get their tickets on the trip to the stars with the Master who returns to pick you up. I have given you an overview that you might not be so foolish as to say there is no such thing as "space men", and a worse one---"These things are of the Devil". That statement, my friends, came directly and blatantly from the Devil himself. How better to keep you from finding truth and help through this horrendous transition?

Now back to "what can you do"? Again I am going to take the liberty of quoting from Dr. John L. King. I highly recommend his advice and a contact place will be given at the ending of this book. Dr. King has never heard of me nor the author; but then, she doesn't know Dr. King so the balance is equal. I shall, however, see to it that he gets this material immediately so he can be expecting any calls which might originate from this source.

Dr. King omits the one most valuable asset you can acquire and utilize, however, and that is the corporation--properly set up, tended and utilized in Nevada with a trustworthy agent or office staff. I will cover it secondly.

So far I have not been able to elicit communication with Dr. King personally so I will take liberties as a Space Commander that you ones should not utilize; that is, using another's material without permission. I trust that since I give him full credit he will be generous with me.

And I quote, "So the question arises, 'What can I do now to protect myself from the inevitable financial debacle?'

And with that, another question, 'How can I take advantage of the bargain-basement opportunities the crash will bring?'" Well, I am not interested in that phase so you ones will have to find out directly from Dr. King.

"First of all, if you persist in believing that Uncle Sam is going to bail you out, or anyone else out, forget it. There is no insurance program in force that will ultimately return your money to your hands. Nor is there any prevention against the domestic social violence that will erupt when financial chaos descends. Nor any way to quickly fix the breakdown in communications and transportation.

"During the early months of the Great Depression, just about everything that could go wrong did go wrong. And now, in the 1980's, there's a whole lot more that can go wrong. Practically everything is hooked up by electronics and computers, so what can go wrong this time will likely go wrong with the speed of light." I would add here that I will, in this document, only refer to maninduced economic disaster. You will also be faced with incredible earth upheavals and changes.

"Second, remember that change is an ordeal. The coming change will be more of an ordeal than previous changes because of its sheer size. It will be far more than financial and economic. It will be political and social, too, for we have reached a watershed in American history. Tomorrow will present a totally new world, which we will have to learn to cope with and fashion a life from. This will be no mere replay of the past. It will be a greater transformation than anything in memorable history". I'm sorry, Dr. King, much different than you can imagine, either.

FIRST, STOP THE LOSS

"What you can do immediately--assuming you are reading this before the crash--is get your money out of banks and S&L's. Don't wind up among the panicked crowd banging on the bank's closed door.

"Also, get your money out of the stock market and out of mutual funds or money-management funds.

"Do not keep more than a bare-bones balance in your bank or S&L, just enough to make a month's worth of bill payments.

"Do not keep money in pension funds, retirement funds or life insurance policies, either. All these institutions invest your money in stocks and bonds and mortgages. Those financial instruments will be hit the hardest, so cash out before it's too late.

"To secure your nest egg, buy U.S. three-month Treasury bills or U.S. savings bonds. The bills are in $10,000 denominations and the savings bonds may be bought for as little as $25. Buy them from your bank's Trust Department or from a stockbroker. The reason this is important is that while all else in the economy can be allowed to disintegrate, the U.S. Treasury will have to be held together at all costs. Without a federal foundation there is nothing at all left. And nothing upon which to rebuild.

"MUNICIPAL BONDS

"This is a favorite haven of everyone because of tax-free income. Present tax law changes alter this wonderful world, but aside from that, cash out of municipals because of a far greater danger: defaults! During the 1930's one of the worst places to have your money was in city and state bonds since so few could honor them. Today there is $1 trillion of this 'paper' out there. Cash out now!

"ALL ABOUT YIELDS

"Everyone wants a high income and this means high interest rate returns that line your pockets. This is especially true of senior citizens living on fixed incomes. They have an imperative to maximize their cash flows with high yields. This is unfortunate.

"A high yield carries with it a high risk. Recently I talked with someone who told me, with some pride, that he still had some big money in a S&L that had been paying him 16-1/2% for 6 years! I suggested that he forget it; S&L's are the worst places in the country to deposit and leave funds because many are insolvent and one day the whole business will go up in smoke. You must be cautious: if you lose your capital, you have no yield, and you are then truly up against it. So, forget yield. Look for capital safety above all!

"U.S. TREASURY OBLIGATIONS

"Right now the best place for large sums of money is 3- to 6-month U.S. treasury bills. U.S. treasury notes and bonds will fall dramatically in price. The bills will, too, but not as far. In addition, you can double your money in Treasury bonds at the right time, which is in motion and coming our way.

"CORPORATE BONDS

"Get out! Too risky.

"CERTIFICATES OF DEPOSIT

Get out! A CD is no better than the bank or S&L that issued it and most of them are in trouble now!

"FDIC & FSLIC INSURANCE

"The FSLIC is insolvent. The FDIC has less than one cent for every $1 you have on deposit. Do not think for a second that the government will ride to the rescue of these deposit liabilities, as many believe. This is because the government must borrow the funds for such a rescue. This increases their debts, which are already sky high, and you would simply pay for this folly as a taxpayer. Not only that; if they even tried such a rescue they would wreck the bond market in the process since foreign holders of U.S. bonds would cash out and destroy bond prices. There is no fast and easy solution to this coming nightmare.

"GOLD

"Start now buying gold coins, any kind, and hoarding them. Keep them at home, not in a safe deposit box at a bank (banks will be closed, and deposit box contents are not insured). Gold will rise to $2,000 an ounce and the bad news is that it will fall back to $35 an ounce. This is because the purchasing power of gold is always constant: one ounce buys a man's suit of clothes; in 1935 $35 gold bought a good suit; today $450 gold buys a good suit. You cannot have a fortune in gold and hope for super-low prices for the things you buy.

"SILVER

"It will rise to over $100 an ounce, and then will fall, too.

"What do you do if you have large profits in gold and silver? How do you preserve your gains? My suggestion is buy land in the country with your profits. Land, of course, will be very cheap as we get further into the depression, less than ten cents on the dollar for most everything.

"LIFE INSURANCE PROCEEDS

"Cash them out now while you can. Why? Insurance companies will take large losses in stocks and bonds and real estate, and pass them on to you. I know this since I worked for a major life insurance company as an economist years ago and saw the debris the Great Depression left. Also, AIDS will finish them off for good.

"PENSION FUNDS

"Pray a lot if you are collecting one. These funds are managed by yuppie whizzes on Wall Street who are up to their eyeballs in stocks and bonds--paper that will vanish. If your pension fund survives, which is doubtful, it will then be cut.

"The stock market crash of October, 1987, directly affected many pension funds, especially those that invested in corporate stocks. Corporate pension funds generally invest 50% of their pension funds in stocks, 35% in corporate bonds, and the balance in real estate, certificates of deposit, etc.

"It is only prudent to find out just where your pension fund has your money invested, and if it is not totally in Treasury bills, try to change this as soon as possible.

"MILITARY RETIREMENT PAY AND SOCIAL SECURITY INCOME

"Both of these will be reduced at least by half, maybe more. But the prices of the items you buy will also fall by that amount, so your purchasing power will be the same.

PRESERVE YOUR CAPITAL

"Above all, you must preserve your capital so you will have purchasing power and income as the economy is stood on its financial head. The good days are gone forever, perhaps, and we are all going to have to do a lot of surviving so you might get ready for this now.

"The large fortunes in America, many of them, were made in hard times or depressions, when the wise and thrifty had funds and bought cheap. In the coming depression everything will be for sale, but few will have saved resources."

I, Hatonn, have been telling my own dear ones this very same thing, and still, some play the "outguess it" game. Well, it is the risk of your lives. That break could come this very afternoon and if so, you will have lost greatly. I mean, you ones who know me well---get yourself under disciplined control; the risk is not nearly worth those few dollars. Besides you will have what you need; better to use it to get in the inner circle where the business can continue to thrive. We intend our cells to thrive.

Ah yes, "WHEN WILL THE PANIC BREAK OUT? AH, IF WE ALL ONLY COULD KNOW?" WELL YOU CAN'T!!

GET, AND STAY, PREPARED

"No one knows when the final, major financial panic will happen. The time is not now that important, but being prepared is crucial. You must be ready. After the crash, it will be too late: you will be licked financially, filled with fear, and unable to cope. I caution you: be prepared. This advice is conservative, but it has stood the test of history for generations and it will tomorrow, too.

"FUTURE BARGAINS IN REAL ESTATE

"Always, in severe deflations, opportunities for real estate buys emerge at bargain basement prices. In Chicago in 1832 during a real estate crisis, a $15,000 house depreciated to $100 in one year. In Florida in the late 1920s a real estate credit bubble grew and then burst, as all credit bubbles do, and beachfront property fell to one cent on the dollar." Well, Hatonn is here to tell you that you are also going to have a rearrangement of your beachfront properties!

"The more palatial the property is, the cheaper it will be since no one wants to get involved with property having high maintenance costs.

"But to take advantage of these real estate buys, you must be liquid. If you are in dicey credit paper, like a certificate of deposit, you stand to lose much of its face value. This makes hoarding gold and silver coins rather attractive, doesn't it?

"The October crash signaled a major reversal in the economy. Until then, the farm, oil, bank and thrift losses and commercial real estate losses had not totally impacted the minds of the public. For some unknown reason, the public maintained an uncanny optimism about the future.

NO HELP FROM GOVERNMENT

"THE STAGE IS NOW SET

"This is the time to batten down your financial hatches and get yourself personally prepared for financial survival. Be self-reliant because no one else will take care of you or protect you, and that includes Uncle Sam, who will have his hands filled, too, with tax revenue losses and larger-than-believable federal deficits and other unique problems.

"For those with an eye to the future, the silver lining and the strategy is to secure your nest egg and patiently await the profit opportunities that always accompany hard times. As in the past most of the public will be caught by surprise, and left standing in a line at the bank. But someone has to be positioned to put Humpty Dumpty back together again. Begin now to become that somebody."

Please hear us, friends, there are several more things I want to take the liberty of pointing out to you. I hope you understand that I most surely am very serious about what I am giving unto you.

If this information is shocking to you, such as the information regarding the world banking "take over", I suggest you continue with serious intent in receiving just a bit longer. If you take care and act promptly you can be spared much of the danger that lurks in the dark. Information and knowledge is your best ally; except for action. You can know all there is to know and yet, if you do not "act", you have garnered naught.

You will have two main enemies in the months to come regarding your financial and self-survival. Your government and your neighbor, for both will become desperate soon enough and, driven by panic, they will both use the force necessary to get what is yours.

INSTANT GOVERNMENT CONTROL

In case you have not heard of Emergency Banking Regulation #1, it is not surprising. You were not supposed to know about it. It is almost impossible to get information about it. Be grateful for careful research in your behalf.

In a "NATIONAL EMERGENCY"--which the President can declare in a time of grave crisis (like any great economic depression)--this regulation gives your government the right to:

CLOSE ALL BANKS.

SEIZE **YOUR** BANK ACCOUNT.

PROHIBIT THE 'HOARDING' OF FOOD AND GASOLINE--AND THEY DETERMINE THE QUANTITY.

RESTRICT AND CONTROL ALL BORROWING OF MONEY.

The imposition of this Regulation will be devastating and destructive to anyone caught in its trap. You must arrange your property so no-one can get at it. They will have the right to do anything legal or illegal, from garnishment to kidnapping to get your resources. The latter has already happened (the kidnapping), by "authorities" during the Reagan administration. Scare you? I certainly hope so!

AVOIDING SOME TRAPS

If you follow some good techniques and instructions you will be able to achieve some security. If you are careless and procrastinating to over-extent you will loose. Pay attention for the time is NOW. If I get inquiries about how to accomplish some of these things, I will take the time a bit later to give you some input. Before I depart this portion, I will tell you a few things that threaten your privacy, your safety and the security of your assets.

Know that your IRS can conduct "informal" inspection of your bank account (s)--WITHOUT YOU EVER BEING INFORMED THEY ARE SO DOING! They gained that right in January, 1989, so if you do not believe me--check it out. Thank Judge Larry McKinney, Federal District Court for that little gem. He ruled that the IRS has a legal right to "informally" examine bank records without a summons, search warrant, court order or even the knowledge of the bank account's owner! As you might surmise, a surprise "informal" investigation is far more effective. You better learn how to protect yourself and get yourself devoid of anything of merit in your bank account.

There is a great misconception that a "low profile" existence is the best way for you to protect your privacy. No---forget it. Do not differ from anyone else--low or high. Fit in the mold and be so routine in appearance that you would not attract a snooper sniper. In a great depression you can't maintain a low profile anyway. Until tax funds dry up and blow away they will have their big guns and magnifying glasses at ready.

Anybody can inspect your credit records--and if that is not bad enough, those records, right now, are probably incorrect. You better get them cleaned up before you have to come up with assets you didn't know were listed, and that you do not have.

Do not count on electronic protection devices to protect. You can count on being under surveillance if you appear to have <u>anything</u> during a great depression. You will be electronically surveiled. Most of my team is already under constant surveillance. There is, however, a rather simple device for debugging --- check with your electronics store.

You must know that the only safe phone is a cellular phone---and it is safe only while you are in motion. It is simple to intercept a cellular phone call, but nearly impossible for a stationary phone tapper to listen in while the caller moves through different zones in the network.

STASHES

Now, I know it is a problem thinking where in the world can you store money around your house and be safe. Well, first of all you learn to put it somewhere and keep your mouth shut. Except, always have at least one family member who knows where to search for things.

For instance, if you bury it outside on your property. Make sure you have watertight, insulated containers and do make a detailed map. You think you will not forget but from season to season and bush to bush you will forget.

Also, your refrigerator or canned goods shelves are quite good--if you weight the cans to be approximately the same weight as the original can with contents.

Your freezer is excellent; especially a large turkey which can be stuffed. But you will have to be careful who accesses these places.

Remove a baseboard in a special room or attic cubbyhole which can be placed back into form with no notice.

Back of a light switch-plate is excellent (within the hollow wall space).

Books which are hollowed out in the center. However, you will be limited, spacewise, if you do the proper thing and get small denomination bills.

Well, I shall have more for you on this later; I want you to have enough at this session to get started! Sit quietly and you will become most creative.
Aho and Amen! This is all I am going to give you from this subject matter for I shall now turn to Corporations. I strongly urge you to rush to the phone or mailbox and obtain Dr. King's material immediately.

Let us take a break, Dharma, as this has been much too long a day for you but time is so precious--each day is truly a gift from here forward. Use it well, my friends. If you pull together as in true community, you can handle this thing come upon you. Divided you shall surely fall. SALU!

CHAPTER 5

REC #1, HATONN

THURSDAY, AUGUST 31, 1989 7:00 A.M. YEAR 3, DAY 015

Greetings, Dharma. May we walk in beauty equal to this wondrous day we have been given. And may our intent be pure, our wording explicit and received in truth. Aho!

Let us just dive right off into "CORPORATIONS". These things must be put forth because your survival is critical to our work being accomplished. You must handle your barter in the most responsible manner. Some of that which I tell you will be so basic it will bore you but I find that most on your place never are given access to knowledge that allows another to be most wealthy.

CORPORATION STRATEGY

I will first tell you what is a corporation. Then I will explain why your state of Nevada is the only state within your United States which I suggest as a home base for your corporation. If you do a business which requires it, you can license within that state. This will be lengthy for I want you to understand, not simply toss aside. I will then give you access to ones through whom you can obtain additional information. Again, I am not in the publishing business nor the incorporation business. I am efforting at saving mine workers' assets instead of having you sitting on them. YOU NO LONGER HAVE TIME TO DRIFT. IF YOU HAVE NO ASSETS TO CONSIDER THEN JOIN WITH A PARTNER AND SPREAD OUT THE ASSETS AMONG CORPORATIONS (KEEP THEM SMALL) AND DO A LITTLE COMMUNITY ASSISTING. If many of you form numerous corporations you can shift assets and divide your hidden fundings and not be placed under inspection by anyone. This will also become clear as I move into describing "why Nevada".

WHAT IS A CORPORATION?

A corporation is a legal, artificial person: a person that is separate, distinct, and TOTALLY APART FROM YOU. It is NOT you. You are NOT it. It is a distinct, different, and totally separate legal or artificial person. Pretend you set up a corporation and named it Samuel Gene. It is the same as if you have birthed a baby boy and named it Samuel Gene. It will have all its own identification. Now as a teaser about Nevada. Suppose the parent (owner) of Samuel Gene wants to hide from public view his (their) relationship as parent -- Nevada is the only state that completely hides ownership of that new baby.

Further, a corporation is a distinct, legal entity separate and apart from its members, stockholders, directors or officers. Although it is a separate entity, it can act only through its members, officers or agents and cannot have knowledge or belief of any subject independent of the knowledge or belief of its people. Woops--your baby has no brains of its own, no wonder you want to hide from the public. A stockholder (owner or partial owner) is a holder of shares of stock in the corporation and is NOT IN LEGAL CONSIDERATION OR DANGER. (In other words you are not, as the owner or parent, responsible for the brain damage). A stockholder is not the employer of those working for the corporation nor is he the owner of corporate property --- IF YOU HANDLE EVERYTHING PROPERLY AND WITH DETAILED REGULATION ACCORDING TO THE LAWS OF THE LAND --- THE STATE OF BIRTH. IF A "FRAGMENT" GETS LICENSED WITHIN ANOTHER LAND THEN THAT PORTION HAS TO FUNCTION WHEREIN LICENSED, IN ADDITION.

A corporation is an artificial person. Its rights, duties and liabilities do not differ from those of a natural person under similar conditions except, of course, where the exercise of duty would require the ability to comprehend or think. That's what the board of directors is for: they do the thinking. Proof that the directors thought on behalf of the corporation is EVIDENCED BY THE RECORDED MINUTES AND RESOLUTIONS. PAPERWORK--YOUR LIVING RIGHTS ARE THE HEARTPLACE OF YOUR NEW BABE--MESS UP ON THE PAPERWORK AND YOU WILL KILL THE CHILD BY NEGLECT. For example, a corporation may become a debtor or trespasser. A corporation can buy, trade, sell and make loans; literally anything you as a person can do.---Think it through. The possibilities become fascinating and you can be most creative.

A corporation is a citizen of THE STATE WHEREIN IT IS CREATED. (THAT IS WHY I INSIST ON NEVADA. SO THAT YOU CAN TAKE ADVANTAGE OF THE BEST CORPORATION AND TAX LAWS IN THE U.S.---LEGALLY AND WITH VERY LITTLE TROUBLE--YOU DON'T EVEN HAVE TO VISIT THE STATE. **YOU 'DO' HAVE TO HAVE A RESIDENT AGENT WITHIN THE STATE OF NEVADA BUT THAT IS PAINLESS, ALSO, THE MONEY IS WELL WORTH THE ASSETS.**) A corporation does not cease to be a citizen of the state in which it is incorporated by engaging in business or acquiring property in another state.

Since corporations ARE SOLELY CREATURES OF STATUTE (LAW), the powers of a corporation in another state are derived from the constitution and laws of the state in which it is incorporated.

A corporation is a legal person which has an existence separate and apart from the stockholders. As an artificial person, a corporation is considered to have its domicile (home) in the state where it is incorporated and the place where it has its registered or statutory resident agent or home office in that state. When the corporation is actually in a different place, the site of its resident agent is sometimes said to be its "statutory domicile".

The existence of the corporation is not affected by the death or bankruptcy of a shareholder or by the transfer of its shares. IT HAS A CONTINUOUS EXISTENCE. IT IS IMMORTAL (unlike you) for as long as it complies with the annual requirements of the state in which it is incorporated (like you when you reach this dimension beyond Earth).

The IMPORTANT POINT to remember is that <u>when you own a Nevada corporation, the corporation exists as a separate entity or person.</u> You can live anywhere you choose, in any state of the U.S., Canada, France, England, Germany, Sri Lanka, Belize, etc., etc. IT IS THE CORPORATION WHICH CONFORMS TO THE REQUIREMENTS OF THE STATE IN WHICH IT "RESIDES". <u>NEVADA, YOU WILL FIND, IS THE STATE WITH THE BENEFITS TO PROTECT YOU AND YOUR CORPORATION. WE HAVE CAREFULLY RESEARCHED IT FOR YOU AND TRAINED ONES ON YOUR PLACE TO HELP YOU THROUGH IT.</u>

NOW, IF YOU DON'T UNDERSTAND WHAT I HAVE JUST WRITTEN---GO BACK AND REREAD UNTIL YOU DO. YOU <u>MUST</u> UNDERSTAND EXACTLY WHAT A CORPORATION IS.

<u>WHAT IS A NEWLY FORMED CORPORATION?</u>

A corporate shell is a corporation that is completely formed and ready to proceed. It is called a "shell" simply because it has NO stockholders, directors or officers, YET. It is a shell with nothing (no life) within it. It has NO assets or liabilities.

It is simply like a brand-new, completed house with nothing and no one inside it. It is simply waiting for YOU to decide what and who you want to put in it, as well as when and how.

<u>Shells are ready to do business immediately</u>. The purchase of an already-formed corporate shell is the fastest, simplest and most efficient method by which you can incorporate, become incorporated, or, literally, instantaneously have an already-formed corporation for immediate use. Further, if you get one of these new "shells" it comes with its birthing certificates and a resident nanny (agent).

Now, Hatonn is not going to give you details about different types of corporations; you can do that work and research for yourselves. There are holding corporations, brother/sister corporations, S corporations, etc., family estate corporations, you name it and you probably can set it up. I have neither the time nor inclination to effort at individual lectures.

WHEN AND WHY INCORPORATE IN HOME STATE (IF OTHER THAN NEVADA)

I will cover when and why you should incorporate in your home state if it is other than Nevada. There are pros and cons.

While that might appear to be complex, the solutions are simple when the subject is understood and the facts assembled.

Keep in mind that the purpose is to take the mystery out of corporations and their use--to strip them of their unnecessary complexities and to make them simple so all can benefit. If you fail to understand, then I have undoubtedly failed to make myself clear and I urge you to research further.

I am not selling anything so I do not intend any type of misleading information, and there are many instances whereby you are better off to simply incorporate in your own state.

NEVADA vs HOME STATE

Let us begin, however, with WHEN you should incorporate outside of your home state (if other than Nevada).

I can promise you that nine times out of ten if you ask your attorney or accountant about these things you will be misled. It is not intentional, it is simply that he or she is usually uninformed and will not risk telling you so. Oftentimes the attorney or accountant does not understand the total ramifications himself and is afraid he is going to lose the individual's business if he does not lead into forming a corporation in his home state.

Of course the attorney or accountant practices in that state and therefore, may keep the individual "locked-in" and, by having that person incorporate in their home state, obviously profit from having the individual "locked-in" regardless of whether it is in the best interest of the individual.

Let me point out something here, before we move away from "out of state incorporations". Most of your large, successful corporations are incorporated in the state of Delaware! (Check on it.) That is because WHEN those corporations were started in business, Delaware HAD the best corporation laws in the U.S. You will find that the majority of the big corporations with whom you are doing business are NOT incorporated in your home state. They are most likely licensed through your Secretary of State to do business within your state. Delaware passed some state laws that now are detrimental to you--for instance, reciprocity of records with the IRS. Nevada never reciprocates information with your federal IRS. Yes, friends, a lot of criminal elements utilize the liberal laws for their benefit---does that mean God cannot utilize the same laws in his behalf? You are required to abide by the laws of the land--go where the laws of the land serve you best. These are man-made laws, they are not against the Laws of The Creation nor of the Laws of God. They are an intelligent manner in which to handle your business in privacy and hold your wealth to bring production instead of abuse unto you.

A corporation is a citizen of the state wherein it is created or incorporated. A corporation does not cease to be a citizen of the state in which it is incorporated by engaging in business or acquiring property in another state. Since corporations are solely creatures of statute, the powers of a corporation of another state are derived from the constitution and laws of the state in which it is incorporated.

Suppose you decide to go live in Mexico, that does not cause you to lose your U.S. citizenship. Further, if the police or neighbors become nasty you can come right back to the U.S. and gain protection. No less with a corporation.

When you are in the original process of incorporating, you probably cannot ascertain whether or not that haven might ever be of value to you. All too often unanticipated problems can arise in your home state, particularly if that state is tough on business and taxes. If your business grows and begins to make a big profit, then it can be nothing short of a godsend or a miracle for the corporation to be able to abandon or abort operations in your home state and retreat to a home base HAVEN: the protection of the constitution of the state under which it is incorporated. It is no accident that Nevada, of course, happens to be the best state in which to incorporate.

WHO SHOULD INCORPORATE?

NOW, I HEAR THE FLOW OF QUESTION # ONE!!??

I AM JUST A FAMILY, OR A SINGLE PERSON, WHAT DOES THIS HAVE TO DO WITH ME?---FURTHER, YOU CAN'T WAIT TO FIND OUT AS HATONN MOVES ALONG--------BECAUSE IT ONLY REQUIRES ONE (1) PERSON TO FORM THE CORPORATION, BE THE BOARD OF DIRECTORS, OFFICERS, THE WHOLE KIT AND KABOODLE (I THINK YOU SAY). AND YOU HAVE **ALL** THE BENEFITS OF A CORPORATION, BUSINESS WISE, TAX WISE -- ALL WISE. WHY DO YOU THINK THE GOVERNMENT SEEMS TO GIVE BREAKS TO CORPORATIONS? BECAUSE MOST OF THE GOVERNMENT "SERVANTS" ARE INCORPORATED (IN THE STATE OF NEVADA) AND DO BUSINESS THROUGH THE CORPORATIONS AND THEIR PRIVATE LIVES ARE NEVER MADE PUBLIC. THOSE WHO BLUNDER AND GET CAUGHT DID NOT. **YES, IT IS THE BEST KEPT SECRET IN THE UNITED STATES OF AMERICA AND ABROAD--FOR ALIENS OF FOREIGN COUNTRIES CAN ALSO INCORPORATE IN NEVADA. THIS IS A BENEFIT THE BIG BROTHERS HAVE MADE EVERY EFFORT TO HIDE FROM YOU**

BENEFIT THE BIG BROTHERS HAVE MADE EVERY EFFORT TO HIDE FROM YOU SO THAT THERE IS NOT A CHANCE OF REMOVING THOSE BENEFITS.

I will refer to "foreign" corporations later also, that term does not mean alien or foreign countries (although it can), it simply means any other "state".

Back to the subject. If, for example, you are starting a small retail business in your home state and you never intend it to become involved in interstate operations or sales, then you are probably well-advised to simply incorporate in your home state. Another example may be a small business where it is reasonably certain that the business is never going to flourish or expand into a much larger enterprise. If taxes become a problem for you in your home state, you may then develop a corporate strategy that will eliminate those taxes. There is a blueprint for that very strategy which I would have made available to you. It REQUIRES a corporation authorized within your dwelling state to be effective. If, however, you form a consulting operation whereby you are not involved taxwise within a state except that you err in living there--you do not need even register the business corporation in your state. RESEARCH, GAIN KNOWLEDGE AND KNOW WHAT YOU ARE DOING--CHOOSE THE BEST APPROACH.

DOING IT RIGHT

Many folks do misunderstand. They often think that they can form a corporation in Nevada, Delaware, or anywhere, and then simply proceed to do business wherever they are. That is USUALLY NOT TRUE! However, each state has exceptions to its legal definition of "doing business within that state". You should find out what the legal definition and exceptions are in your state and act accordingly.

If the law in your home state legally defines your business as doing business within that state, then you must either incorporate in your home state or qualify your Nevada corporation, or any other out-of-state corporation, to do business in your home state. In other words, simply because you have formed a corporation somewhere does not necessarily permit you to do business everywhere (without qualifying to do business in each additional state or else being legally exempt from qualifying or registering). You must determine what the regulations are in your state.

However, as example, a Nevada corporation can own property in ANY state without having to qualify or be incorporated in that state. Therefore, in this instance (owning or buying real property), you are exempt from incorporating or qualifying to do business in your home state. When that circumstance also exists, then you would certainly want to incorporate in a preferred state and let that corporation in the preferred state own the property. That means any real property. Then if you sell the property--simply sell the whole corporation. Many benefits in that kind of transaction, my friends. Have a little genuine fun--find out about these things that are hidden from you behind the hypnosis of mundane T.V. and your "death" existence. Simply determine what activities are exempt from qualifying to do business in your home state and those which are not.

LET ME GIVE YOU A LITTLE PROOF AS REGARDS FEES IN CALIFORNIA. IT COSTS SO MUCH TO INCORPORATE DIRECTLY IN CALIFORNIA. IT COSTS ABOUT HALF AGAIN AS MUCH TO QUALIFY TO DO BUSINESS IN CALIFORNIA FOR A "FOREIGN" CORPORATION (LET US SAY, NEVADA). THAT IS BECAUSE CALIFORNIA KNOWS THE VALUE OF THE INCORPORATION IN A SEPARATE STATE AND USES THE FEE TO DISCOURAGE YOU. I SEE A GREAT ADVANTAGE TO INCORPORATING IN NEVADA AND PAYING THE DIFFERENCE IN YOUR HOME STATE TO QUALIFY----PRIVACY--IN NEVADA NO-ONE KNOWS WHO THE OWNERS (STOCKHOLDERS) ARE. EVEN IF YOU MUST QUALIFY IN ANOTHER STATE THAT INFORMATION CAN USUALLY BE KEPT PRIVATE EXCEPT FOR THE PORTION OF YOUR CORPORATION ACTUALLY DOING BUSINESS WITHIN THE QUALIFYING STATE.

It is wise to incorporate in the state with the best corporation and tax laws regardless of where you are going to do business. Then, if for ANY reason you ever wish to, you do have a safe HAVEN, as it were, to return to or retreat to or withdraw to. YOU WILL HAVE TO HAVE DONE YOUR BOOKWORK IN PERFECTION TO KEEP THE CORPORATE VEIL FROM BEING PIERCED---HOWEVER, FRIENDS, YOU ARE GOING THROUGH THE GREAT TRIBULATIONS OF ARMAGEDDON; CAN YOU NOT DO A BIT OF WORK IN YOUR OWN BEHALF TO MAKE IT THROUGH IN WHOLENESS?

I do say that incorporation is a very tidy way to organize and get the best breaks around, wherever you choose to utilize the tool. Nevada is the most overall efficient state for personal incorporations for dozens of reasons. I shall not bore you with all of them, for information is available in detail. I will prevail upon one of my workers who can receive mail and phone calls and direct you to these resources, at the end of this manual.

HOME STATE BUSINESS

As a last definition on this subject: A corporation is only authorized (licensed) or allowed to do business in the state that it is incorporated in (obviously for tax purposes); <u>unless</u> and until it is qualified (or exempt from qualifying) to do business in another state. Remember, the corporation is a "foreign" corporation in every other state except the state in which it is incorporated.

To qualify a "foreign" corporation in a state is many times referred to as registering or licensing the corporation to do business in the single respective state in question. The terms all mean the same thing and are usually referred to as "to qualify" or "to register".

To qualify or to register in a particular state usually requires that the particular state be paid a one-time qualification or registration fee. When the fee is paid, that foreign corporation is then recorded in that particular state and is therefore qualified or registered to do business in that particular state.

Also, a requirement in practically every one of your states--AND VERY IMPORTANT--is that before the corporation can be registered or qualified, it must have a resident or statutory agent appointed (which is for service of process) and, of course, that resident or statutory agent has to be duly appointed and accept that appointment on or with the papers filed in that particular state.

The other requirement for qualification or registration in any state (in addition to paying the required fees and having a resident agent) is that the name of the corporation desiring to be registered may not already be in use in that state by some other corporation. If the name is already 'taken' or in use in that state, then the corporation cannot qualify with the real name assigned to it by a 'foreign' state. However, not to worry, the corporation in question is still allowed to qualify by registering as DBA (doing business as) a name NOT already taken or in use in that particular state.

Let us take a break, Dharma. I realize this is most tedious for you but it is most important that mine co-workers and associates clearly understand. I do not function as so many of the touted ones from "outer dimensions". You ones ask for, and need help--not more words of doom and disaster. You will have enough of those, even from me. I am telling you what to do NOW to gain as much protection as you possibly can. Whether or not you choose to utilize the information is not for my deciding---mine is to give you alternatives to losing it all. No more and no less. So Be It! I move to standby and await your summons to proceed. SALU. Hatonn to standby. Out.

CHAPTER 6

REC #2, HATONN

THURSDAY, AUGUST 31, 1989 1:00 P.M. YEAR 3, DAY 015

Hatonn returned. Let us proceed rapidly, Dharma, for a few days saved at this particular point can mean tremendous difference in outcome. Again, I am getting this information to my people--if others find it useful and helpful, blessings. I intend to neither defend nor unduly explain. I understand that your question is; "Well, why bother, time is out anyway." Well, we are going to treat corporation management exactly as if you have the next ten thousand years to do business exactly as today. If you act too late, it's just too late. If you can utilize this even one or two months it is well worth the expense and exercise. I will go one step farther in the subject of "doing business" in a state. Each state will have its own regulations but I will quote a brief section from the California code to example:

BUSINESS EXEMPT FROM QUALIFICATION

"Without excluding other activities which may constitute transacting business, <u>a foreign corporation shall not be considered to be transacting business solely by reason of carrying on any one or more of the following activities.</u>

"1. Maintaining or defending any action or suit or administrative action.

"2. Holding meetings of its board or shareholders or carrying out other activities concerning its internal affairs.

"3. Maintaining bank accounts.

"4. Maintaining offices or agencies for the transfer, exchange or registration of its securities.

"5. <u>Effecting sales through independent contractors</u>.

"6. Soliciting or procuring orders either by mail or through employees or agents or otherwise where such orders require acceptance without this state before becoming binding contracts.

"7. **Creating evidences of debt or mortgages on real property.**

"8. <u>Conducting an isolated transaction within a period of 180</u>

days and not in the course of a number of repeated transactions of like nature."

WHY INCORPORATE?

There are a multitude of strategies and useful personal assets to be utilized by no other method. You can minimize risk by protecting yourself.

The tax rate for corporations is now less than the tax rate for individuals. This alone usually justifies incorporating.

To be incorporated enhances your ability to raise funding.

If you simply incorporate you gain personal protection and limited liability. If you do so in Nevada you compound that asset.

You can set up your estate and it can be totally and completely handled much more safely, efficiently and economically by incorporating. You may save all the legal expense, probates, legal entanglements and traps connected with probate. You can totally protect your loved ones. This is through the incorporation and then the specific and proper issuing and setting guidelines on the "stock". In other words; you can die and leave a mess. Corporations never die, they just get a new president and go right on doing business. No interruptions, just new management.

Here is a grand one for those of you on social security (for as long as it lasts), and also wish to continue in employment. You may draw your maximum social security benefits AND allow your corporation to earn as much as it possibly can without being penalized for earning or making money.

Incorporating creates orderliness and efficiency. You need to keep accurate records and I will insure you learn where to go and obtain any necessary information.

Corporations are the most effective tool available in real estate matters of buying or selling, and also owning and managing. I request all of mine ones get all of this information for you will be handling much real estate. I am going to request that whenever possible you have property incorporated prior to any purchase of it so that you are dealing in corporation buying, selling and exchanging rather than real estate.

WHY NEVADA, HATONN?

One good reason: There is a law, enacted in Nevada (which few other states have) that protects directors and officers from personal liabilty for acts committed on behalf of the corporation or by the corporation. Nevada is a pro-business state and has enacted laws that are far more liberal than laws in any other state in your Union. This is for the sole purpose of encouraging prospective incorporators to come

Nevada HAS NO FRANCHISE TAX. NO CORPORATE INCOME TAXES. NO PERSONAL INCOME TAX. NO CAPITAL STOCK TAX. NO STOCK TRANSFER FEE OR TAX. NO TAX ON CORPORATION SHARES. NO SUCCESSION TAX.

STOCKHOLDERS AND DIRECTORS ARE NOT REQUIRED TO LIVE IN OR HOLD MEETINGS IN NEVADA. SUCH MEETINGS MAY BE HELD ANYWHERE IN THE WORLD. NEVADA ALLOWS CORPORATIONS TO DETERMINE WHAT KIND OF STOCK WILL BE ISSUED. NEVADA LAW ALLOWS BY-LAWS TO BE CHANGED BY DIRECTORS.

**INITIAL OR MINIMUM CAPITAL IS NOT REQUIRED. Further, if you follow my suggestions and utilize the Agent I recommend you can be shown how to enhance your capitalization by tremendous amounts without outlay of very much cash investment.

MAINLY, YOU GET ANONYMITY--PRIVACY--SECRECY OF OWNERS OR STOCKHOLDERS. FOREVER.

THIS IS ALSO A MOST IMPORTANT POINT: In Nevada you have minimal disclosure and reporting requirements. Only names and addresses of officers, directors and resident agent are required on an annual basis. There are intermediary ones available who will substitute in for you annually so that even those names are kept in security from public record--all perfectly legal through the Nevada Secretary of State. BUT YOU HAVE TO KNOW WHAT YOU ARE DOING!! AND YOU HAVE TO DO IT RIGHT!! SO DON'T PLOW FORTH IN IGNORANCE AND BLOW YOURSELVES AWAY--GET THE REQUIRED INFORMATION TO DO IT RIGHT. THAT IS PRECISELY WHY I WILL TELL YOU NO MORE ABOUT THE PROCEDURE FOR I DO NOT WANT YOU TO "CHEAP" IT AND FALL IN THE MUD ON YOUR FACE. IF IT IS WORTH DOING; DO IT RIGHT. IF YOU DO NOT DO IT RIGHT--PLEASE FORGET HATONN'S NAME IN THE TELLING OF THE FAILURE TALE. ONE IN MY LITTLE CIRCLE HAS A SAYING: "IF A THING IS WORTH DOING--IT IS WORTH DOING!" WELL, IF YOU DON'T INTEND TO DO IT RIGHT, FRIENDS, LEAVE ME OUT OF YOUR BLUNDERING.

BEST OF ALL: ONE (1) PERSON CAN DO THE WHOLE THING! SO BE IT AND AMEN.

If I could get every one of my workers to do what I would really enjoy, it would be to have at least three corporations for every man, woman and child. Any corporation which reaches the size to be noted would break off into little corporations and just continue to conduct business among its fragments. (All separate and distinct.) You would also only buy or sell to and from corporations--keeps government tabs to a minimum or absent altogether.

ENEMIES?

Dear ones, if you are to make it through the times ahead of you, you must be at least as clever and diligent as your enemies. And who did I tell you are your most dangerous enemies? The government and your next door neighbor, unless he happens to do what you do. And then you are squarely up against Mr. Satan---face to face. That, however, is another story and covered elsewhere--or very soon will be.

Beloved ones, you are to and into the end times of a world evolution. Naught will be forced upon you by any of our realms. Interference is not allowed by Universal Cosmic Law. We can participate only to the extent requested and at this point, that will be only through these means of communication. Soon it will be through interchange of presence---when safety is assured. At this time you are the hands and feet.

Simply put in a more important format: YOU ARE THE BODY OF GOD MADE MANIFEST UPON YOUR DENSE PLACEMENT. YOU WILL HAVE TO DO IT FOR YOURSELVES. WE WILL ASSIST AND HELP FOR WE CAN SEE THE ENTIRE OF THE PICTURE AND YOU CANNOT. YOU HAVE BUT TO HEAR AND RECEIVE OF US.

Esu Jesus Immanuel Sananda is the overall commander of this project and my advice to one and all----HEED CAREFULLY THAT WHICH IS BROUGHT FORTH UNTO YOU. IT IS YOUR TICKET HOME! WAIT TOO LONG AND YOU SHALL BE LEFT WAITING FOR THAT WHICH WILL NEVER COME, FOR YOU WILL HAVE MISSED IT!

As Hatonn, my duties are more of a physical, practical nature--your physical survival and transition. Immanuel is gathering of His own and any who will accept of Him. We all serve in the Command of God, Aton (the ONE total Light) within the totality of The Creation.

HANDBOOKS OF SURVIVAL

These projections will constitute your instruction manuals. You will only be charged that which is the cost of printing and distributing the material. THESE CAN BE CONSIDERED YOUR HANDBOOKS FOR SURVIVAL. IF YOUR BROTHER CANNOT AFFORD ONE, DO HIM A FAVOR, GET HIM ONE ALSO. GIVE A REAL "CHRISTMAS" GIFT. GIVE THE GIFT OF INSTRUCTIONS FOR THESE DAYS OF TRANSITION. THERE WILL BE SOME MOST WONDROUS REVELATIONS COMING FORTH IN PROPER SEQUENCE AND YOU WILL BE GIVEN TO KNOW THE TRUTH OF IT.

Dharma, I need no postscripts to this document save the information of contact for information. Please ask the ones who format the document to make sure that information is placed properly within.

I have carefully studied and watched the ones whom I utilize and can only qualify those ones for accuracy. I trust there are other ones who can act in some instances, i.e., "resident agent", but the one I will recommend is totally trustworthy and can give you the added assistance a novice will require.

I place my seal upon these words and information. As a forward (introduction), please utilize the information of identification of myself.

Because you ones must become familiar with the recent appearance of Jesus Immanuel Sananda I request you place his picture within these final pages. I do not wish to shock you but you will realize that when he appears to gather up his flock, he will be well trimmed and in a command suit---you ones better get used to that image. His hair is now shorn appropriately but his general appearance is as the likeness herein. So be it. You are being prepared for the final days and the coming of your cosmic family. Immanuel Sananda will not longer stand aside for your foolishness. I plead you practice wisdom.

I stand aside now, in infinite love and appreciation. I must rely on my close receivers and workers to see to it that information to specific questions be handled from there, unless it becomes necessary for me to write an addendum. We have so many other matters to cover that I believe you have enough to go forth and take ACTION! Linger on the handling of your economic affairs and you will be too late. YOU ASK TO BE TOLD--TO BE WARNED. HERE IT IS LOUD AND CLEAR AS ONE OF THE TRUMPET BLASTS. NO "IF"---IT "IS". OPEN YOUR EARS AND HEAR; YOUR EYES AND SEE!

I AM COMMANDER GYEORGOS CERES HATONN TO SIGN OFF.

BLESSINGS IN THE TRIUNE OF POWER

SALU * SALU * SALU

CHAPTER 7

REC #1, HATONN

SATURDAY, SEPTEMBER 2, 1989 6:30 A.M. YEAR 3, DAY 017

SURVIVAL PREPARATION

Greetings, Dharma. There is a most indispensable subject yet to be covered in this little do-it-yourself book. It is "survival" preparation. Again, it will be brief. There are publications on your market which are excellent for survival information so in this journal I will speak of DO THIS NOW. We plan to give you detailed further instructions in forthcoming dispatches but for this manual we just want to keep you alive and fed for a short period of time until you can add to your supplies. I cannot urge you greatly enough to ACT IMMEDIATELY-NO MATTER WHERE YOU RESIDE OR WHAT YOUR LIFE STYLE MIGHT BE.

OBERLI, MAKE USE OF THE SECTION ON EARTH CHANGES, FROM SIPAPU ODDYSEY, OR FROM SISTER, ADDED IMMEDIATELY FOLLOWING THIS CHAPTER. IT DEALS WITH U.S. CHANGES AND IT IS COMING DOWN RAPIDLY. THE WRITINGS WERE GIVEN IN ALMOST VERBATIM WORDING TO BOTH DHARMA AND SISTER----THAT, FRIENDS, IS FOR YOUR CONFIRMATION OF 'OUR' TRUTH. AT THE TIME THE DOCUMENTS WERE WRITTEN, THERE WAS NO CONTACT BETWEEN THESE TWO RECEIVERS. SINCE DHARMA'S WRITINGS WERE FOR DIFFERENT INTENT AT THAT TIME, YOU MAY FIND SISTER'S TO BE MORE COMPREHENSIVE. I WILL TELL DHARMA WHERE TO LOCATE IT. (Please refer to Chapters 8, 9, 10, and 11.)

Our intent is to assist as many of you ones as is possible, wherever you reside. Most ones will be within cities and therefore most of the survival books are not instantly helpful.

You, especially in earthquake zones, tornado troughs, hurricane areas, volcanos (even dormant--they are all going to erupt) need waste no time. The weather patterns are already changed greatly--that will intensify beyond your ability to comprehend. Therefore, you will be having droughts and floods in the most unlikely places.

You are headed for oil shortages which in turn will hamper transportation. Ultimately you will have periods of days without electric power, gas availability and clean water supply. The cities will be hit worst in this instance.

Oberli, get Sipapu Oddysey ready for printing as soon as possible. It is written in fantasy format -- but, it is truth and carries "timing", changes and other information acceptable to non-"believing" readers. Let us please move right along with that project. I believe Eilsie and Philus are working on it already. Yes, its thrust will be in a major motion picture but the information needs to be filtering out there NOW!

I am hereby asking Dr. King, Harley Laughlin and Merlin Sampson to recommend these books from ASSK in their newsletters--you are on the ragged edge and ready to fall over the cliff. WE must get word to the masses and get them to ACT! These books will be offered, as with your items, at a price only to break even for those responsible for the printing, etc.

Here I am going to suggest some books to get immediately: THE EARTH CHANGES SURVIVAL HANDBOOK, by Page Bryant, Sun Publishing Co., P.O. Box 5588, Santa Fe, New Mexico 87502-5588 U.S.A. It is $20.00 and worth every cent. (I will be covering the information later, but if you can share the book among a few of you---get it and do so. NOW!)

FIGHTING CHANCE, TEN FEET TO SURVIVAL, Arthur Robinson, Ph.D. & Gary North, Ph.D., American Bureau of Economic Research, P.O. Box 8204, Ft. Worth, Texas 76124; $5.95. This is the most important survival truth you will ever have. Utilizing these informations you can then move on to building a community action and save many, many ones from death in your dimension. It requires "COMMUNITY" however, not just a group of people---I speak of "community" as Dr. Scott Peck speaks of community---I will do an entire manual on that subject very, very soon ---sorry, Dharma. (Please understand the stress and unbelievable work load for this little scribe and be patient---we will get it done as quickly as possible. Often I will refer to good publications that we might relieve her in the interim.)

WASTE NOT TIME OR FUNDS

NOW, THERE IS SOMETHING I WANT TO POINT OUT TO YOU THAT IS OF UTMOST IMPORTANCE. YOU WILL FIND TRUTH IN THESE BOOKS AND YOU WILL FIND MUCH ADVERTISING FOR OTHER BOOKS. BECAUSE I ASK YOU TO GET A BOOK FROM A PUBLISHER DOES NOT MEAN I APPROVE OF THE PRESS OR PUBLISHER. ANY "METAPHYSICAL" NEW AGE BOOKS ON CRYSTALS (OTHER THAN FOR BASIC USE), ASTROLOGY, ASTRAL PROJECTIONS, CELESTIAL CORRESPONDENCES, ETC., ETC., - DO NOT WASTE EITHER YOUR TIME OR FUNDS. THERE IS NAUGHT BUT YOU AND GOD, FRIEND, AND SITTING A CERTAIN WAY, OPENING UP YOUR RIDICULOUS CHAKRAS, CHANTING AUMS, PLOTTING YOUR STARS, ETC. ARE THINGS OF CHILDREN'S GAMES--NOTHING MORE!

YOUR PHYSICAL FORM IS SIMPLY A HOUSE FOR YOUR SOUL. A VEHICLE. IT WILL RUN BETTER IF TENDED--IT WILL NOT AFFECT YOUR SOUL. YOUR SOUL WILL CHANGE DIMENSION ACCORDING TO ITS GROWTH AND LESSONS ACCOMPLISHED---BETWEEN YOU AND GOD. PHYSICAL ACTIONS IN INTENT OF PERFECTION ARE NEGLIGIBLE UNTIL YOU CLEAN UP YOUR CONSCIOUSNESS. YOU WILL MAKE THE TRANSITION INTO HIGHER DIMENSION THROUGH GRACE, NO OTHER WAY. WHERE YOU GO IN THE OTHER DIMEN-

SIONS IS ACCORDING TO YOUR SOUL GROWTH, NO MORE AND NO LESS. SOUL DOES NOT KNOW DEATH, ONLY TRANSLATION. DESTINATION OF TRANSLATION IS DETERMINED BY YOUR SPIRITUAL RELATIONSHIP TO THE CREATION AND CREATOR. SO BE IT. THIS IS NOT THE FORMAT FOR THESE PARTICULAR LESSONS.

I SAY THESE THINGS FOR I WISH NO MISUNDERSTANDING: IF I RECOMMEND A PUBLICATION OR LESSONS FROM CERTAIN ONES. IT MEANS **EXPLICITLY** THAT! FURTHER, I DO NOT EVEN AGREE WITH ALL IN ANY PUBLICATION, SAVE MINE OWN, AND OTHERS FROM MY INNER GROUP; THEREFORE, USE INTELLIGENCE--I RECOMMEND THESE BOOKS FOR THEY HAVE LISTS AND QUANTITIES, ETC. FOR SURVIVAL OF THE HUMAN CREATURE IN THE MOST EFFICIENT MANNER.

SOURCES

Merlin Sampson, P.O. Box 396, Midvale, Utah 84047, 801 561-5615 can make available to you a "Buying Service" whereby you can purchase, at great savings, items for survival needs, foods, lighting, tools, etc. He can give you information where you can get a package which will provide bare necessities (save personal items, sleeping gear and water) for a family of four for 72 hours, for instance.

He has agreed, through Dr. King, to offer the service at a third the cost of regular membership. Through him you can obtain information regarding all survival elements.

I SUGGEST YOU MENTION DR. KING WHEN YOU CALL OR WRITE TO MR. SAMPSON; AS WELL AS MENTION THIS PUBLICATION FOR IT WILL BE THROUGH THESE RESOURCES THAT YOU WILL GET THE BEST POSSIBLE PRICING AND PURCHASING ABILITIES.

You need the best pricing for I suggest you have a longer supply of foods than for 72 hours. You need a minimum of 7-10 days. Los Angeles, for instance, will be without basic ability to function for much longer than ten days.

Los Angeles and the coastal cities of California are going to be effectively cut off from basic services for quite a period of time----AND YOU ARE HANGING BY ONE VIBRATIONAL TONE FROM THE BIG ONE COMING DOWN THE FAULT LINE. WHEN IT GOES, SO PROBABLY, WILL GO SOME OF YOUR RING OF FIRE VOLCANOS. IT IS GOING TO BE ONE BIG MESS, BROTHERS.

If you can truly only afford one "GOBOX" (Ranos, make sure a duplication of the page on "GOBOX" is included in this material) then at least get one. You need two. You will also need additional items for support to the kit. Extra fuel for the little stove, a gallon of water per day, sleeping "bags" and a supply of personal items. I would wish you would have one of these kits, with water, in every vehicle you use, every outing you take. It might very well be your survival.

It is not nearly enough, however, for in emergency you will be impacted by ones around you who have naught. I am sorry, brothers, it is time long past, to be prepared. You are in the final stages of the countdown to Armageddon. We have been sent into your space to give you instructions. Let us come into truth and acceptance rapidly for you must get prepared or perish---the time grows very, very short indeed.

For you ones who can make it to safety outside the impact area and find yourself "on the land", I suggest:

The Bear Tribe's Self-Reliance Book, The Bear Tribe Publishing Co., P.O. Box 9167, Spokane, Washington 99209.

Within these books, you can learn what you need and where to go for the items. ACT TODAY, DO NOT WAIT---YOU MAY VERY WELL BE TOO LATE BY THE TIME THIS INFORMATION COMES INTO YOUR HANDS. IF SO, PRAY THAT YOUR NEIGHBOR HAD IT AND ACTED TO INCLUDE A FEW WHO ARE UNPREPARED.

To keep the burden from these ones in this place until they are better organized, I request that calls for information be funnelled through ASSK in Sedona, Ariz. For those of you who know who this receiver is and the location, may, of course contact these ones. You will, however, on this date find they don't have all your question answers. I give Dharma only that which you all get to protect her until I can be insured of her safety. Obviously, these ones will have more information for I will have them obtain these books and materials as soon as possible. In fact, Dharma, I want you to immediately get these publications, in your area you need the Bear Survival Book.

I wish to thank one, Alice Tebbets, for making available the book "FIGHTING CHANCE". It will save uncountable lives for it is both an expose' as well as extremely practical. As we move along we will be introducing earth compression machines that will allow you to excavate and utilize the excavated earth to build your bunkers.

MAKING LEMONADE

It does not need to be a dreadful experience; it is a challenge and those who respond and act will actually have it very pleasant and quite comfortable.

We will then need take it further into the communities and build some model accommodations. There is no reason that you cannot have a safe haven (under your school play yards, parking lots, parks, etc.) for comfortable survival for all of your community and handle influx of transients. The cost can be most reasonable and the comradery of such a project is a wondrous experience.

I will make an effort to get my ones to obtain a supply of these books or at least allow for the placing of orders for all, through one outlet at ASSK. Be patient while ones gear up for the project. You must, as the public, understand that the information coming forth from these places causes great impact on the ones involved. They, like you or any of your friends, serve US and run daily lives, jobs, etc. This is a service of love and gifting to you fellow humans. WE will keep it as easy as possible for you ones, however, for we have learned it is the only way the human kind responds---if it is no effort and does not interfere with fun or ego. You have a long way to go friends, pray you have the time for you are in grave circumstance. LOOK AROUND YOU -- THE END TIMES ARE ALL AROUND YOU! I do not carry a placard that tells you next Thursday at 10:00 A.M. your world will blow. Anyone who does so, is a blatant liar. I do tell you the transition and all the accompanying trauma is in your dooryard! You have less than twenty years to the ultimate "biggy"--that means you only have a brief time to prepare. When I say BIGGY---I MEAN VERY LARGE!

Let us close this now, Dharma. I have given only the brief outline but it must suffice for there are more urgent needs for your time presently. Ones must wake up and take responsibility for themselves. This is to wake you up--the alarm clock is ringing. Open your eyes and take some action to save your own fannies for there is not anyone else to do it for you. To believe you will be tended is absurd; you will save yourselves or you will not be saved. So be it and Aho!

Let him who has ears to hear--hear and eyes to see--see! Otherwise, continue to sleep and dream but be prepared to wave goodby to your friends who do see and hear. It is not enough to believe Christ died for you on a cross and all you have to do is believe it. Faith without works is naught. Works without intent of truth is naught. You better brush up on truth of the way it is and not based on the lies you have been fed. SO BE IT AND I PLACE MY SEAL UPON THE TRUTH OF THESE MESSAGES. SELAH.

Let us take a break, Dharma. We are doing fine, chela. You ones are greatly blessed for we know how stressed the path.

SALU HATONN TO STAND-BY OUT.

TRANSITION

THERE CAN NO LONGER BE A SEPARATION OF THE PHYSICAL MAN FROM THE SPIRITUAL MAN LEST THERE BE SEPARATION OF SOUL MAN FROM GOD.

DO NOT DWELL ON "WHAT WAS" OR LINGER IN THE "WHAT IF". YE MUST KNOW AND ACCEPT "WHAT IS" FOR TRUTH AND KNOWLEDGE IS BEING LAID BEFORE YOU.

IT IS A WISE MAN WHO RECOGNIZES TRUTH AND ACTS ACCORDINGLY.

The following four chapters are added as a guide to the survival of the soul; in the end, more important than those chapters foregoing

CHAPTER 8

REC #1 ESU JESUS SANANDA

TUESDAY JULY 25, 1989 7:00 A.M. YEAR 2, DAY 343

FOLLOWERS OF LUCIFER

Peace and light are yours, thank you for attending my requisition. Today I will speak of things most momentous, which will sit like lead in the bellies of millions who believe they act and learn in truth. Even the great ones of Christ ability to fortune miracles, have marched through the ages, formed cults and are deadly to thy "Christ" teachings. Just as today, ones have come in falseness in the name of Holy Creator God but are against you and other cults as well. They are in service, in truth, to the fallen Lucifer --- who, ye must remember, was above all other creations in the Father's kingdom; birthed in perfection.

I do not pronounce villainy upon the followers, as they are of the masses who simply follow, but it is why ye must be most selective in the study of any doctrine ye take unto you for those ones are terrorists, in the major portion, and the "good" men are trampled over. I speak of these things for it will give you background to understand what will come to be in the present sequence.

THE TIME OF MY CRUCIFIXION

I will speak of the time of my condemnation to crucifixion, briefly, that you might better understand my words. At the time I stood before the people, many of them claiming to be mine own, they began to denounce me. It was at the time of Easter. (Ye better not misunderstand the meaning of "Easter" as used at that time. It was a most widely celebrated pagan holiday.) At Easter it was a tradition, the governor (at that time, Pilote) was accustomed to releasing one prisoner, whomever chosen, except when one was guilty of murder or of a death. Any other crime accusation was not considered.

At the time I was put before the crowd there was another prisoner named Barabbas.

When the crowd had gathered for the "show", Pilote spoke to them, "Which one do you want me to release; Barabbas, the criminal, or Immanuel, of whom it is said that he is a king of wisdom and the son of an angel?"

BUT HE KNEW THAT THE HIGH PRIESTS AND THE ELDERS HAD PERSUADED THE PEOPLE BY GIVING THEM COPPER, GOLD, AND SILVER SO THAT THEY WOULD ASK FOR THE RELEASE OF BARABBAS AND TO HAVE ME KILLED.

He knew very well that I had been taken and turned over because of envy and hatred since my teaching was liked by the people. Also, and beware of this next for it is no different today; my beloved friends, thy very families will betray ye if they desire in negative intent. His WIFE brought great influence to bear upon Pilote for his was a political and power filled position as governor. She urged him, "Do not have any dealings with this just man, because today I suffered greatly in my dreams on account of him and find his teachings are good." Pay attention, in this instance she was the one who did not condemn but, equally as deadly, she asked him to withdraw justice in decision.

Pilote asked the gathered crowd, after they chose to release Barabbas and contain myself; "What shall I do with him who it is said is Jmmanuel, a king of wisdom?" You see, there were many choices in the hands of Pilote -- just as there are many choices always resting in thy own hands.

The people screamed: "Crucify him. Let him be crucified."

But Pilote was not willing to do such drastic action and asked very angrily, "What evil thing did he do so that you want him to be crucified? He only taught a new doctrine and for this he shall suffer death?"

But mass chaos had set in (beloved ones, there are always the frenzy mongers who propel the masses), and the shouting became a chant.

PILOTE WASHED HIS HANDS

Pilote saw that he could do nothing against the crowd of incited people who had been persuaded and that there was great unrest and turmoil. He took a pitcher of water and washed his hands before the people and said, "You decide for yourselves that which you will do with him. He is the captive of the elders and the high priests, so let them judge him. I have nothing to do with this just man, for I am innocent in regard to him and hereby wash my hands before you in innocence." How many do this in hopes they won't be blamed for indecision; how many of mine very own ones do it daily unto me? Are your courts any different in the very cases you have pending before a justice bench? If you are ruled against; or, the enemy is given jurisdiction -- how do ye fare in the outcome? Worldly treasure wins almost constantly in thy place - either man is not willing to back thee or will actually sell thee out to hold his own treasure -- which is God's anyway. So be it, the choice always lies within the individual. The shame and remorse was horror to witness within the individuals following that day. "I" was not denied and crucified; thy "GOD" was denied and crucified---ponder it carefully friends for it makes great, great difference to you, even here in the America. THE DEBTS WILL NOW BE PAID!

I was turned over to the priests and the elders and was whipped and bloodied that they might somehow indicate my "crimes" unto the people. They put upon me a purple robe to mock my "royalty" in order to ridicule and degrade. They placed thorns in my hair and wreathed them about mine forehead whereupon they beat them until the blood blinded mine eyes. They spat upon me. They "dared" Father God to do anything unto them in my behalf. Well, perhaps some will wish I could not be in the remembering of their labels for many will be set to the straight. KAIPHAS, the high priest, mocked me, saying, "So, what are you going to do now, you great king of wisdom?" How many times might you stand in similar circumstance and make a wrong choice? Ye have the power to pulverize them and ye have to make of a choice. I chose silence for no other choice was left to me; I could denounce publicly mine Source and negate the very reason I was sent forth, or I could take my stand for all mankind. Ye will also be put to the test over and over and over---ye have been. Your presence here at this time in sequence indicates ye failed the test at one time or another.

Not so much will be asked of you in physical pain but much will be asked of you in courage and hard decisions and in giving of your "all" back unto the giver of all. The amounts will be of piddling nature but represent the entirety of decision.

Ye are asking "proof" of me. I see it in thy minds constantly so do not bother to cover and hide. I am going to remind you of several things I said on that day of hate and rebellion against God.

MOHAMMED'S COMING PROPHECIED

I recall they hit me until I could not stand nor see and I could keep mine silence no longer. I said unto them,, "As you beat and mock me, you too shall be beaten and mocked. The time will come in FIVE TIMES ONE HUNDRED YEARS when ye shall atone for this day. A NEW MAN WILL RISE UP IN THIS LAND AND WHIP AND PERSECUTE YOU, AND YOU SHALL HAVE TO PAY WITH YOUR BLOOD. HE WILL CREATE A NEW CULT AND HAVE PEOPLE CALL HIM A PROPHET, AND HE SHALL PERSECUTE YOU THROUGHOUT ALL TIMES. EVEN THOUGH HE WILL BE A FALSE PROPHET AND BRING YOU A NEW FALSE DOCTRINE, HE HAS GREAT POWER AND WILL HAVE YOUR RACE PERSECUTED THROUGHOUT ALL TIMES TO COME. HIS NAME WILL BE MOHAMMED AND HIS NAME WILL BE,

FOR YOUR KIND, HORROR, MISERY AND DEATH, AND YOU MOST SURELY DESERVE IT. VERILY, VERILY I SAY TO YOU, HIS NAME WILL BE WRITTEN WITH BLOOD AND HIS HATRED AGAINST YOUR KIND AND LINEAGE WILL BE ENDLESS.

HOWEVER, SINCE HE WILL BE A FALSE PROPHET AND BRING YOU A FALSE DOCTRINE, SO WILL HIS CULT EVENTUALLY BE FINISHED, WHEN YOUR KIND AND HIS KIND WILL PUT DOWN THE FOUNDATION FOR A BLOODY END.

DO YE NOT THINK THESE THINGS CAME TO PASS EXACTLY AS STATED? LOOK IN THY REFERENCE BOOKS IF YE REMEMBER NOT. I AM NOT COME TO TEACH YE THY HISTORY MANUALS. I AM COME TO RECLAIM MINE FATHER'S KINGDOM AND MY BROTHERS, WHO HAVE WALKED MINE PATH OF WHATEVER COLOR OF SKIN OR LABEL FOR CREATOR SOURCE.

THE TRUTH WILL BE HEARD

Ah yes, other PROPHETS have been sent forth and persecuted for always has the truth been hidden and the lie continued for how else could the dark force hold power? So laws have been written and rewritten in an attempt to silence the seers of truth. Attempts will be made again, to silence this scribe and she prophecies not, for all I give is already written - - - - but, THIS WILL BE HEARD THROUGHOUT THE LANDS, MAKE NO MISTAKES ABOUT IT, BELOVED ONES, AND IT RESTS WITHIN YOUR HANDS AS TO WHETHER OR NOT YE SUCCEED AS INDIVIDUALS IN THY TESTING. YE HAVE NO WAY OF KNOWING WHO THEY ARE OR FROM WHENCE THEY ARE SENT, THIS OBERLI AND DHARMA, FOR THEY DO NOT YET KNOW IN CONSCIOUSNESS. YE, AS INDIVIDUALS, WHO CLAIM DESIRE TO PARTICIPATE IN THIS ULTIMATE PERFORMANCE, WILL PROVE OF THINESELVES UNTO ME. SO FAR, THEY HAVE MOSTLY HAD TO WORK ALONE AND FACE EXTREME ODDS AGAINST PREVAILING IN A MOST WORLDLY WAY IN WHICH ONES OF THE CIRCLE COULD COMPLETELY RELIEVE THEM OF THE CROWN OF THORNS AND THE LEGAL BATTLE. SO BE IT. YE CLAIM TO BELIEVE; THINE ACTIONS DO NOT INDICATE SUCH. (STOP OF THY GAMES, DHARMA, YE DO NOT DOUBT OR YE WOULD NOT BE HERE, CHELA --- YE ARE CONSCIOUSLY AFRAID IN THE PHYSICAL SENSE; YE ARE NOT IN "FEAR". KNOW THE DIFFERENCE FOR IT IS OF GREAT IMPORTANCE.) ALL OF YOU, KNOW THE DIFFERENCE! BETTER YE BE IN FEAR OF GOD THAN MAN!

PROPHECIES

I shall utilize some prophecies already brought forth unto you that this one not be in jeopardy.

"The Antichrist very soon annihilates the three, twenty=seven years his war will last. The unbelievers are dead, captive, exiled; With blood, human bodies, water and red hail covering the earth." Not a very pretty picture of your future is it? "Near the harbor and in two cities will be two scourges, the like of which have never been seen. In the years to come, hunger, plague within, people thrown out by the sword, will cry for help from the great immortal God--!"

The war itself would not need last twenty-seven years, brothers, it requires at least that time for the radioactive atmosphere to clear enough for life. Ye are destined to be surrounded by a radioactive belt in thy atmosphere which will be as great as any radioactive orb in the universe. Thy planet is destined at it's end -- it's dense format, to be a sun about which other planets will orbit.

Did not the potential for such desecration come forth at Hiroshima and Nagasaki in thy sequence years of the 1940's?

The "third anti-Christ" is in place, beloved ones. IN PLACE! FURTHER, IN PLACE AND READY TO "BLOW".

1996

"When weapons and documents are enclosed in a fish, out of it will come a man who will then make war. His fleet will have traveled far across the sea to appear near the Italian shore." This indicates a probable lining up of the planets you call Mars and Mercury and are in conjunction with Pisces, that will be in your year 1996 on March 23rd, as thy astronomers predict, I believe. Look for a big year in 1996, brothers, for the prophet goes on: "The Oriental shall come forth from his seat, to pass the Appenine Mountains to see France (Have I not told ye ones to keep thy eyes on the Euphrates river also and look for it's drying? Ye have a severe drought of massive size today. How many years of severe drought does it require to dry a magnificent river?). He shall pass through the sky, the waters and snow, and shall strike everyone with his rod."

1999

This beloved seer has told you that in 1999 and seven months a powerful king would come from the skies. So be it, so be it. These foretellings were sent forth only four hundred years ago when thy calendars match pretty well, today's. Here is wisdom, little ones. Let him that hath understanding counter the number of the beast: for it is the number of man; and his number is 666. It is also 999 depending upon thy perspective. Also, ye can expect an intervention from the direction of "Mars" - - and where travels the starship Bethlehem?

"After great misery for mankind an even greater approaches --- WHEN THE GREAT CYCLE OF THE CENTURIES --is renewed, it will rain blood, milk, famine, war and disease: In the sky will be seen a fire, dragging a trail of sparks." This will represent the Wormwood of thy Holy book. It will be the relief orb for a great migration of Earth people. Great damage will be inflicted on the place of America for there will ensue an age of "nuclear winter" whereby the sun is darkened and no thing can grow. Ye ones will either be prepared and withstand the time of massive deprivation or ye shall be secured elsewhere until recovery necessary for safety in thy returning.

THE SEVEN YEAR COUNTDOWN

Ye will very soon be watching for a second "sun" to be visible. It will be noted and will remain visible for some seven days of your timing. This will be a sign unto mine ones that thy seven year countdown has begun. Ye will know 'tis ME.

As ye ones in receiving of this directed message are within the United States of America, I shall share some other prophecies of this great seer which were removed and forbidden circulation by the political wardens.

"In the West, blood runs in streets, night screams out. A populace outraged. Men in warrior garb strike out; Security dies. Victims battle helplessly, but the warriors are supreme in a new dark age of terrible chicanery." Ah so - - - ?

Is it not so that ye are in the midst of crime in thy country that it is like the rockets into thy sky - - - out of control and out of reach of rectification? Criminals will strike out against helpless victims everywhere and the elderly will be targets for the thieves and the blood flows in the streets as the criminal gangs, even unto the children, kill and mutilate. Your law enforcement agencies no longer can contain nor buffer between the criminal and the citizen, especially in thy cities of density. The population will be outraged, but also powerless to stop the hordes of savages who will descend on you with their guns and knives.

And why? "The second millennium minus ten, in the West, multitudes in vertigo. Disorientation reigns among all. A flower to blame. Graves overflow with the young. A royal decree fails and leaders among the ruins. Contamination is everywhere; the land, air and sea is spoiled. Invisible clouds descend on the multitude, unaware. Insidious death. Sickness. Engines of power grind into red dust, acid from the heavens, and a universal color fades."

Pretty blunt without my input isn't it? Have ye not a population almost totally dependent on drugs? Narcotics as ye call them will replace alcohol liquor and will cause millions to perish from abuse or crime association therewith. Do ye not think ye are headed to this irreversible point by thy 1990? Do ye not note the pollution which grows daily? The people of the earth will be sick most of the time as ye move along for ye poison thy air with particulate that floats upon the air currents for thousands of miles. Acid from the heavens? I think this needs very little comment.

What of the engines of power grinding into red dust? Well, suffice it to say that when ye have no fuel to run thy factories, machines and other energy-burning engines, ye will cease to be able to use them and this commodity will become so valuable that much bloodshed will happen. Ye will turn again unto the deadliest of all -- nuclear, and by this time the criminal element and abuse of substance will be so great that the invisible cloud will contaminate thy country in widespread measure. The physical bodies will deteriorate from radiation poison and it will seep into thy water and thy food stuffs. The blue color of thy heavens will be clouded and distorted by all manner of products.

The flower referred to is the hemp plant and thy opium poppies from whence comes thy most addictive narcotics. Ye are in it, beloved ones, do not hide thine eyes---YE ARE IN IT!

TREASURIES SINK

What of: "The Occident reels. A new revolution, bloodless, engulfs the multitudes. Levies oppress. Leaders quake as the royal coffers are bare and great gold treasuries sink and a comet two years past has crossed the sky." ?? When did Halley's Comet traverse thy skys? Would it by any chance have been in 1986? What would two years past indicate? 1988 perhaps? Treasuries sink? Debtor nations out of control --- thy own in certain collapse --- open thine eyes! Do ye not think the levies will be more and more oppressive? There will be a day when the people can no longer pay of taxes and an overwhelming revolt of non-payment will strike your nation. All thy reserves of precious metals (gold) shall be taken from thy storehouses and exhausted in an attempt to save of thy government political center. It will only purchase of thee a tiny bit of "time", it will not alter the course of the path.

THE FALL OF ISRAEL

Let us now consider for a moment, the state of Jewish Israel which ye ones saw fit to reestablish in thy 1948. "A spit of land in the midst of sand and water arms itself against mighty hordes. Robed men descend enmasse masse. Thunderbolts. Lightning. The arrogance of the few melts. Blue waters claim a once powerful nation."

So be it and Selah! Look to your maps. Look to the state of Israel and cast thy minds to that which has already been given unto you even this day. Ye will see in the MidEast, that Israel is really a spit of land with water on one side and sand on the other. It has armed itself against the enemies it has, and is the fourth largest military might in the world in your day. The robed ones will descend upon her and all the arms available cannot save her. Nothing is enough against the hordes of robed ones descending on her. Thunderbolts and lightening are the weapons of war. Israel will be lost and then those who participate will be driven into the ocean - - - - and so it will continue!

DELIVERANCE FOR MOTHER EARTH

Beloved ones, little is the world of men; small indeed is the Earth---yet precious in Our sight, for the Earth surely is a willing servant of the Lord. For long has She been in bondage, and long has She suffered. Long has She served in the capacity of the Footstool of the Father; for long has She served in the capacity of asylum and laboratory, and She is now in quarantine, yet she shall be delivered out. She shall be cleansed and brought out of bondage, and once again She shall send forth Her radiance into the forests of the universe; She shall be a shining orb. She shall bring forth a new generation, and it shall serve The Father and therein She shall know great joy and there will be great rejoicing within the heavenly realms. I tell you surely, the Earth has travailed long in Her sorrow and pain. Now She shall be delivered up.

She shall be delivered up. Be aware of Her travail and be prepared to share Her joy. Be ones which have suffered and pained with Her and ones which shall also be delivered, for it is now come when the Light shall consume the darkness, and the Light shall go forth and all creatures shall be made new. They shall be as they were created to be, for they shall no longer be as the ones bound in darkness. This is mine word upon which I place mine seal this day.

Ye shall rise as on wings of dawn and you shall have the Rod of Power, and it shall serve you true and well. Be as ones in alertness and let peace be within you. MINE PEACE I GIVE UNTO YOU THAT YOU NOT PULL FROM ME IN FEAR AND TRIBULATION. I AM THY ROCK. SO BE IT AND SELAH.

I AM THAT I AM. I AM ESU JESUS IMMANUEL SANANDA

I SHALL FERRY YOU THROUGH THE PASSAGE

CHAPTER 9

REC #1 ESU JESUS SANANDA

WEDNESDAY JUNE 28, 1989 6:00 A.M. YEAR 2, DAY 316

Esu Jesus Sananda present, Dharma. Thank you for being in the receiving of my humble self.

Ye of little faith, how shall we prevail if ye doubt and doubt and doubt? Ye gather a new portion from afar and ye fragment and scatter of thine energies. Ye proclaim "powerful" and "wondrous" and hold ones ye know not in esteem.

NO NEW PHROPHETS OR PROPHECIES

I have told thee "there are no new prophets or prophecies". I say unto you that you had best tend thy business and stop of thy "squirming". I make no comment regarding the new recordings ye have brought into thy presence. It is but a rehash and taking of documentation from the scribing of Sister Thedra, my beloved handmaiden. Ones take of the words and pretend them to be great new and wondrous revelations. They are not of newness, these words of the one Douglas Schoeffler. He has but drawn maps of that which precious Thedra has brought forth. Further, it is also documented in the pages of Sipapu Oddysey and the portions which were set aside in order to shorten of the pages.

Ye marvel and ye astonish and ye pick of thy location upon a map drawn and quartered by another and pronounce yourselves over-flooded. So, I ask of thee, what is in newness? Have I not said unto thee that ye will be isolated upon an island? Do ye believe I do not care for thee? Do ye believe I would not send a boat for thee?

We are in the preparation to come in mighty numbers as your preparations for war and holocaust are being formulated behind thy visions. We are in the standing by in readiness to loose ones of other time bands. Ye and they, will be gathered up and relieved of the terrible experience of the mighty holocaust of those events which will come to pass in thy time. We are prepared; are ye ready? Nay, ye talk and talk and ponder and marvel ---- ye are not ready! Ye will be where ye will be, brothers, ye will be where ye shall be. NONE WILL ESCAPE THE TRANSITION; MUST THESE THINGS BE REPEATED AND REPEATED UNTO YOU? HOW LONG BEFORE YOU LISTEN AND HEAR MY WORDS?

My most beloved, Sister, wrote of my projections in thy years just following thy decade of the fifties. In the third year she became my most confident scribe and by mid year of thy 1954 she was projecting in perfection that which would come to be upon thy place. Ye ones do not do of thy homework, for it all is available unto you if you would but seek it out of the shelves. Ye ask and ask of me to give thee more; there is not more ye need except to do of thy work and find what is already about thee. Why do you think Sipapu is of importance? It is to bring these very truths to thy attention in the most abundant manner. Stop of thy lamenting and get on with thy works as outlined before thee.

There are things of earthlyness that must be performed within the areas of the map of Douglas S. Ye have been given detailed reasons why ye will be in safety in Tejas Shape' and if ye believed upon my words as prior given, ye would immediately see the errors in his mapping and projections. Why do ye choose to believe a stranger who has only projected that which he came by by way of Thedra? Let go of my hand and ye let go of thy life source, chelas, and I am vexed with thee.

The cyclic time is at hand, no more; no less. What is told unto you that is new? The cycle has come to full circle. There shall be a mighty awakening in the days ahead, it has already begun. It is only that ye do not hear or pay attention until thy clock is late for you choose to sleep on and ponder that which "might" come. I will repeat all of it here on the pages that ye can see of it again, then ye can make choice of thine own mapping. But I warn thee; do not effort to out-think thy brothers of the Higher Planes for ye will be tended if ye do as bidden; run helter-skelter and ye shall bring upon self destruction. Ye have agreed and accepted the task at hand, do ye leave of me now upon the word of a human? A human who only takes from that of my scribe?

ONLY ONE PLACE OF SAFETY

There are many ones to whom this information is given forth and as the similarities come into thy attention; pay great vantage unto it for its confirmation, not its difference and perceived danger. Do not project of maps with lines which represent death of the body or land mass lest ye be caught in the trap of perceived doom. The great promises are already brought forth, it is only for you to understand their meaning and continue with thy works for the time is at hand and ye must come into balance. There will be no place in which you can proclaim "safety" ---- only within MYSELF! I AM THY SHELTER AND I AM THE WAY AND EXCEPT BY ME NO ONE SHALL COME UNTO OUR FATHER. HIDING NEATH THE ROCK OR WITHIN THE CAVES WILL DO NAUGHT FOR NO PLACE SHALL REMAIN UNCHANGED. THY WAY AND THY SAFETY IS WITHIN MINE HANDS AND I AM OF A MIND TO BE TENDING OF THEE. SO BE IT, COME AGAIN INTO THY BALANCE AND PLACE NO MORE ATTENTION UPON THESE STRANGER'S WORDS. YE HAVE OF ME IN THY PRESENCE AND IT IS TIME YE COME

INTO UNDERSTANDING AND COMPREHENSION FOR YE SADDEN OF MY HEART THAT YOU DO NOT RECOGNIZE OF MY PRESENCE.

FROM THIS DRAW THINE OWN MAP

I have told thee that in thy country of the United States, it will be rent in twain in the area of the Mississippi River and the region of Canada, the Great Lakes as you call them, and that river shall be split to the Gulf of Mexico, into Central America and all that environ shall be changed.

The land to the West will be as a great sea and therein shall the Lotus bloom once again. The times of the fulfilling of these things are close at hand, brethren. The "Land of the Lotus" is the great land which was submerged thrice and then was remained beneath the waters of what ye call the Pacific Ocean. Just as she was cast into the fury of the deep, she will rise likewise in the glory of the new dawning as a new order and a fertile land. When this is in accomplishment, the mid area of thy country shall be as she, sunken into the sea with only a few of thy highest mountain acropolii left as islets; perhaps three and no more than five. After the waters settle there may be a few scattered more. These shall be in the area of the Atlantic Ocean.

Further, to the areas of the Atlantic; the bottom will submerge the land of the seaboard. The risen land will be as a new mountain range of the eastern portion; rugged beyond thy comprehension as to reflect the mightiness of the Himalayas; they will stand at the highest point some 18,000 of thy measured feet in altitude, and the land will bear the city of the old for the scientific ones to explore. That land will be cold as thy present highest peaks and uninhabitable. This particular mountain range shall extend unto the Equatorial belt.

That which is known as England will be as naught seen; the place of France will be to the bottom of that which is now the Atlantic. The great place known as Russia will be a sea as that one now known as the Black Sea and the Mediterranean. To the north it will flow as one into that which is known as Siberia.

There is no law, brethren, of the earth that will change a hair of it or cause it to be stayed.

NOW HEAR ME WELL, CHILDREN OF THE HUMAN AND ELDERS OF THY RACES, HEAR ME WELL. THERE WILL COME, AFTER ALL THESE THINGS COME ABOUT, A RESTING OF PLANET EARTH FOR SOME 3,000 OF THINE YEARS. PEACE SHALL BE AS CALMNESS AND SOLITUDE OF QUIETNESS UPON THE SURFACE OF THE BLESSED EARTH TO THE ENDING OF THE CYCLE, THEN SHE WILL AGAIN BE PEOPLED AS FROM THE FIRST, WITH THE ONES FROM THE PLANETS OF THY SOLAR SYSTEMS. THERE ARE SOLAR SYSTEMS WITHIN SOLAR SYSTEMS IN THE OMNIVERSE. **YE ONES OF MINE FLOCK**

ARE HERE AT THIS CLOSING OF CYCLES TO CAUSE AND ASSIST IN HER WONDROUS TRANSITION INTO HER RIGHTFUL PLACE OF GLORY AND TO AGAIN BRING LIGHT UNTO OUR FATHER'S CREATION ----- UNTO ALL LIFE FORMS.

I COME TO RECLAIM

NAY, THERE IS NO LAW UPON THY PLACE WHICH CAN STAY THE HAND OF THE CREATOR FOR HE AGAIN SENDS ME TO RECLAIM OF HIS CREATIONS. I COME NOT AGAIN AS ONE TO BE DEALT WITH LIGHTLY; **I COME AGAIN TO RECLAIM THAT WHICH IS MY FATHER'S AND THAT WHICH IS THY FATHER'S HEIRS. I SHALL MEET MY FALLEN BROTHER AND I SHALL PREVAIL. THOSE WHO CHOOSE OF HIS DARKENED PATH SHALL BE CAST INTO THE VOID WITH HIS ANGELS.**

YE OF MINE ONES SHALL BE LIFTED UP INTO THOSE CRAFT WHICH RIDE THE WAVES OF THE ENERGIES OF THE UNIVERSE AND REST UPON THE CLOUDS OF SPACE. I WENT FORTH FROM YOU TO PREPARE A PLACE FOR THEE; THE PREPARATIONS ARE IN READINESS. WHO OF YE WILL COME WITH ME?

Those ones who will serve as thy rescue workers are trained well. There are multitudes of the rescue workers and ye shall do of thy portion from the land masses. Ye are not back upon this place to play of thine own fun and self-centered games; ye are here to do thy appointed work that man will not perish as a species upon this beloved orb. OPEN THINE EYES AND STOP THY DICKERING AND SILLY PONDERINGS. TRUTH IS AFRONT OF THEE; STOP LOOKING FOR IT UNDER THINE BUSHEL.

Yes, the ocean waves will wash over those lands of desert sands and roll upon the new shores of the mountains of the great Rocky Mountains --- this new and great tide of the Pacific. The land will be drenched THOUGH NOT SUNKEN-----but, the great places of the Coastal lines will be no more.

Ah yes, there will be ones who will awaken to find their beds aflooded by those mighty Pacific waters. This will be the lay of the lands awash with the ocean and will run the distance from thy Washington State unto the coastal areas of Chile whereupon the great and mighty waves shall roll in unto the Mountains of Rock. Those great places that ye now know as the coast area will be no more.

Ah yes, brethren, thy rescue workers are mightily trained. In our command will be the light forces (that which are recognized as light beams). We utilize the light beams as a magnetic impulse to bring into such impulse as the frequency demands. We will be given whatever level of energy light forces of cosmic energy necessary for such transportation into the safety of that craft readied unto your needs. This science is not unknown unto thy knowledgeable scientist but the impulse timing of light force is not comprehended. I, Sananda, shall be in control of the timing of the bands unto the various densities.

The place of the desert will be an open place for the "Timeless Ones" to take up their charges. For they will be in number to be as numerous as a great flock of birds. Whither man will go he will know not for they must be grouped and herded into the prepared craft. They will be as the dead of the floods and mighty upheavals; the dying will then cry out in terror and hysteria unto the Christ --- why must man wait until his perishment to petition for his transit? None shall escape the upheavals; why do ye wait?

CALIFORNIA?

Let us speak of that place within the United States called by ye ones as California. There will not be a place within that State which shall be as is, for there shall be a great purging, and a great overflowing; teeming and seething of the masses beneath the waters, and a great sinking of that which is above; not a place shall be left untouched within the earth. But there shall be areas of protection whereby the land masses will be thrust upward into an altitude above the onrushing waters. Islands will be left thrust above the waters. The seed of the beginning will be kept in safety for the replenishment of these portions. Ye who trust of me not, shall find yourselves in great conflagration. Ye better be getting thy beliefs into order and cease the inner sparring. Which shall it be, brother? Which shall it be? Great numbers of ones shall find themselves swimming in their beds----and the whirlwind shall catch them up. So be it, for it is so.

Wherein shall ye turn for safety in the days of the great upheavals of the greatest magnitude the world has ever known? It shall be in the fulfilling of this law within thy time, precious ones. I remind you that no person who has gone the last mile will be mid the great cataclysm, therefore, no person will be in the wrong place, nor shall he be in another other than his own place; and it shall be the right place. I shall know wherein ye are; I shall know. Ye ones of mine rejoice for within the ocean bed lies the cradle of the next generation upon the earth and ye shall see it come to be if ye walk with me. Ye can walk within the calm stillness of mine protection if ye but come with me. But take yourself away and into the fray and ye shall find "hell".

There shall be such a great rush of winds and great upheaval of the earth and the greatest of all, the fire from earth within shall leap from beneath. It shall be as a molten mass and ye shall be glad to be on the mountain peaks. The havoc and storms will be most mighty in that place of Los Angeles in the California. There shall be thousands upon thousands who are homeless and in great tragedy and it shall extend Southward and Northward all the length of the coastal areas.

AND MORE

Then shall come the great force from within the earth which shall be as a parting of the land, which shall be from the North to the South; and it shall be between the North Sea and the Gulf of Mexico; and it shall be in the time when the trees shall bow down their boughs unto the ground.

There will be such mighty winds as to wipe away all the places which are now standing with the radius of the great open places which are know to you as Oregon and Washington of the United States. The winds shall increase and become more and more great until they impact the great mountains ye call the Rockies; then they shall change direction and move into the lands of New Mexico, Arizona and Texas, and they will destroy most of the towns of greatest size to be known as cities and villages. Therein shall it blow and blow, taking many lives. So many of them have been unto themselves traitors and traitors unto Father Creator.

The Earth shall be thus renewed, and she shall be made new, brethren, and she shall be within a new posture but she is not to be destroyed for she is in rebirthing. She will no longer and in no wise be as the old, for she shall be made to shine in all her glory for she shall be renewed in the cleansing.

Dharma, enough for this portion for ye are "undone". I request that ye be not about earth matters this day for I must commune with thee. Oberli can be about the matters of business and contacts for this is thy job, chela, these things must be repeated for even those who have read the words sent forth in priority have forgotten. So be it and selah. Man will awaken or man will perish for naught will change of the tides. Man has been told thus for eons of time that they would know that which would come to be: it is written that there would be pestilence, there would be famine and there would be horrendous war. And they shall call for peace but where shall they be in the finding of peace? They shall be as one which has no place to lay of his head and they shall make their beds in holes, and they shall be as the burrowing creatures seeking protection from that which will come upon them. So be it for it is written in the Word.

I SHALL NOT BE IN THE FORSAKING OF THEE FOR YE ONES ARE MY BELOVED AND I SHALL WALK WITH THEE UNTO THE ENDING OF THE CYCLE FOR YE, TOO, ARE ABOUT OUR FATHER'S WORKS. SO BE AND SELAH; BLESSINGS IN THE LIGHT OF OUR HOLY CREATOR/CREATION; THAT WHICH IS ALL UNTO ALL.

I AM ESU JESUS SANANDA OF THE GOLDEN RAY OF CHRIST
IN HUMBLE SERVICE TO MY MOST REVERED FATHER AND
UNTO YE OF MY BROTHERHOOD. I AM THE WAY,
THE TRUTH AND THE LIFE.

CHAPTER 10

REC #1 ESU JESUS SANANDA

THURSDAY JUNE 29, 1989 6:00 A.M. YEAR 2, DAY 317

I AM ESU JESU JESUS SANANDA AND I COME WITH MY FATHER, ATON GRANDFATHER --- THE I AM PRESENCE, THE I AM THAT I AM. THIS DO I SAY THAT THERE BE NO MISUNDERSTANDING OF WHO I MIGHT BE FOR I AM!

TO SISTER THEDRA

Dharma, I first give credit where credit is due; to ones who have walked long in the path and have done my bidding in love and truth; humility and obedience. I will speak only one, chela, for she has walked with me so long and waited so patiently. I honor and cherish beyond thy boundaries to understand, my scribe and my friend; the one known to you only as Sister Thedra, for her name is written boldly in the book of life. She is most human. Ye do not need put on false purity and pious faces for my workers need strength and endurance, perseverance and determination; not pseudo credentials.

NEED YE TRUMPETS?

Ye will now abide with me that we might put to paper some reminders to follow on from the day past. Ye are in the remembering for I come in the reminding. I have the clarions with me, would that make thee hear a bit more clearly if the trumpets blow in thine ears?

The time is upon ye ones of Earth when ye may wait very little more. Man will hear and act, or man is in grave, grave circumstance. He either moves on or he will be left to the elements of the Earth. They shall consume him as the physical matter of flesh that he is. That portion eternal shall take upon itself another format and it shall be sealed. He shall have no memory of that which has passed his attention, and the experience of the past shall be wiped from the screen of his memory.

Not a human person shall be as he now is. They will take a new garment and also a name of newness, for it is given to man to be as the little children. He shall then be given to grow into that which he yet knows not of, for he has not yet become as God; and he shall be within the Law when he proclaims that which is his station. Within the time which is allotted unto such things, he shall become as God and become God in Oneness. He will be given to know all and he shall be allowed expression for he will have knowledge, for it is given unto man to murmur the murmurings of the unknowing and unlearned and that which is misbegotten and bastardized, and it profits him naught.

Man shall learn that which he has said shall be as his bindings. He shall be indentured by his works until they have been fulfilled unto every jot and tittle. He shall become as one who has within his grasp the scales whereupon he may weigh the words; all!

Not any other shall be responsible nor represent excuse for the actions of self. That which is done by another will be answered by other, for it is the law that no man atones for another; yet it is the law that each shall love his brother as himself. But, each will stand naked and alone at the reckoning. When the sorcery is removed he shall awaken unto truth and acknowledgement of that which he is.

AS THE ONE DEAD

Man will find that he has descended into Earth in its darkness, and he has taken upon himself the clothing of the Earth, and he has absentmindedly misplaced his true identity with the Father which sent him forth. He has not only been dreaming, but he has been worse than asleep, he has been as the one dead. It is given unto man to believe that which he sees, feels, and touches is "real", and yet he knows that which he cannot see exists, and without question does he enjoy the benefits thereof; yet he has not been in the least concerned with that which shall profit him most, for it is for his own good that these things have been given unto him. He has failed to follow and perpetuate that which is eternal, for it has been given unto him to be as the human physical being.

The physical sees, feels, tastes, and hears that which is of the Earth, and that which is eternal and without the flesh he sees not, neither does he hear. He shall be blinded and deafened unto reality until he has grown to the age of accountability whereupon he shall then receive his inheritance which is vision and sound. For then shall he be given to understand and know that which his vision perceives and his ears receive.

NOT A PERSON WILL DENY THAT WHICH HE DOES NOT UNDERSTAND OR COMPREHEND, FOR THEREIN IS THE GREATEST OF FOLLY AND TOTAL FOOLISHNESS. **THERE ARE NOT ANY SO FOOLISH AS THOSE WHO THINK THEMSELVES "WISE"!**

Within the time at hand many truths of newness, shall be learned. He must prepare himself for that which shall come unto him. He shall be as one lost in the darkness; yet there shall be lamps of light which shall be sent unto him that he may have beacons to follow. My lamps shall be lighted as they are found; lighted from the candles which I have given unto the bearers.

I AM THE WAY

It is said that "I AM THE WAY," and it is so! None can come save by me, for I am the keeper of the gate and the guard at the door, and I guard my secrets well. Not a person is so foolish as those which plunder mine secrets. Man is given to take that which he can steal and pilfer without paying the price. Therein is folly! for is is the law: that which is earned is for the best part worth the works, and that effort is within itself that which is most profitable and bears merit unto thee. It is for this reason that much is kept from man -- that he might increase and decrease strength and that he may learn to stand alone within the time when there is not help for him. Yet, there is no time when help is denied; but the wisdom of withholding it is the greatest of all good deeds that a man might reach fine stature.

Oh, precious ones, there are those who would "purchase" their fare into the place called Heaven where they perceive they might obtain a life of ease which should profit them naught. That which is not profitable unto eternal life is denied them by the Father, for He knows before they call, that which they need and that which shall profit them and matches within the heart place the mission of purpose of the soul.

Attend well now, chelas, these words for they are of great import.

AWAKE TO THE REAL

It is time to arise from their sleep and shake the dust from the bedclothes. It is time to awaken and become alive. THEY SHALL LEARN THAT WHICH IS WITHIN THE LAW AND BECOME AWARE OF THAT WHICH IS REALLY "REAL". They shall cease being bound by the garments of the flesh; for it is the Law: that which is eternal surpasseth that which is flesh. That which is eternal is not bound within the flesh, and it has never entered into the flesh--yet flesh has its being in that which is eternal, without beginning and without ending; no more and no less. So it is that the flesh shall pass, and the ONE WHICH "IS" shall not be less for its loss.

In the days which shall come there shall be a great gathering in; they shall be separated and shall be as ones of old. They shall be as the sheep and shall be herded into places as the flocks of the fields ---- for it is given unto many to follow. There are few who dare to stand apart and take exception from the crowd. But, 'tis he who takes his stand and says for himself which way he shall go, shall find his way and therein, friends, is wisdom if thy way be that of truth. There are none so foolish as those who sit and wait for the masses. For the masses know not the way.

FAMINE AND PESTILENCE

And so shall it be in the days which shall come forth; for there shall be great famine and great tribulation, pestilence and great suffering; it shall be as naught seen yet before. Not a solitary place shall be left untouched. That is the outward manifestation of that which shall be, for it is written in the Law; that which goes out must come back. It is given unto man to be the part which has gone out from the Father, and to the Father he must return.

In the days to come, therefore, there shall be a great gathering together as ones await one who dares assume responsibility for them; and it is a poison indeed. When it is given unto him to prove himself, he has not the strength to withstand temptation and the tribulations which come forth. He has been unto himself untrue by passing on unto another the responsibility which is rightfully his own.

So shall they learn the path of hardness, for it is the Law that each in his time shall become that for which he was created to become; yet there is naught "time", for that which ye have created as "time" is not within the Law; it is an illusion of man.

RUN FROM THE SUN

And yet, the "time" is at hand when there will be magnificent changes, rebirthing, tribulation and meeting of responsibility. For the Father has sent them which have guarded the Earth for her duration, and they have NOT been sleeping. They have not forgotten their identity, for they are trustworthy and they have been entrusted with the guidance of the Earth and her destiny. She has not gone awry for naught, nor has she been on an orgy of man's definition, for she has gone the way of her ORDAINED COURSE; and it is for the good of all that she shall move out into a new berth (place); for from her solar sun shall she run, FOR THEREIN IS DANGER WITHIN THE FUTURE; FOR IT IS GIVEN UNTO THE ORB WHICH YE CALL "SUN" TO EXPLODE WITHIN ITS ORBIT. In this, there is great wisdom, for the sun has fulfilled the cycle which was ordained unto the sun.

Within the place wherein the Earth shall move there shall be a new solar sun and a new orbit shall be given unto the Earth. She shall have no darkness for it shall be a new field within the firmaments. A new berth shall be given unto her, and the time element shall be new unto her, for there shall be no dark shadows within her. She shall be given a new sun and a new moon. She shall have no pains to bear and she shall be given into rest. She will be brought forth again into youth. Ah, she shall shine forth in glory and she shall be peopled with ones which have awakened and those which shall remember that which has been gone before. They shall be ones with the Father, and shall know that which is of the Father and that which is of Earth.

THE AWAKENED ONES

Therein shall they abide within the Law which is of the eternal. They shall not be bowed down with the pity of the Earth as it is now upon the Earth, for it is indeed pity to see them which stirreth not; they walk with eyes blinded and they are deaf unto the call of the Clarions, which have been sent unto them for their own blessed sake.

Within the time which is at hand they shall see and they shall hear, and they shall be as one which knows not what he sees; yet he shall call out for learning, and it shall not be denied unto him. Many are among them for the purpose of bringing unto them the light and truth and it shall not be withheld from them, however, neither shall it be forced upon them for force is ungodly. All must choose freely, his path.

Within this time come upon thee, they may be the children of the Father, yet there is great forgetfulness as to the way unto the Father's dwelling. They shall cry out for assistance and roadmaps and, it shall be given unto them freely and without price. DO YE HEAR ME? WITHOUT PRICE --- FREELY GIVEN. SO BE IT; CAUTION TO THOSE WHO WOULD DENY THY BROTHER ENTRY UNTO TRUTH AND THE PATH TO FATHER'S HOME. JUST AS THE ABUNDANCE IS GIFTED IN RETURN TO THOSE WHO FREELY GIVE, SO SHALL THAT BE TAKEN AWAY IN MEASURE TENFOLD FROM THOSE WHO DENY MY BROTHERS ENTRY.

Now it has come upon the Earth that which man has feared, and known within with great dread, that which he understands not; and he cries out in his delirium that there is no place for him to hide wherein he will not be found.

Not a person shall say it is not so, for therein is folly. That which is created shall fulfill its cycle and return to its native state. The time is come when the Earth shall move out into a new placement, she shall have a new orbit and both a new sun and a new moon. She shall then be given into resting before being again given unto peopling and a time of beginning again. She shall be restored unto newness. And, those who will be sent shall be a new people, and they shall know that which is of the Father. There shall be a new Garden, and there shall be the Father's kingdom upon the Earth. There shall be the one who will reign supreme, yet man shall work as "one" in harmony, peace and love.

Ah yes, there shall be peace. Each man shall be peace unto himself, and he shall be as the keeper of the peace for all. He shall be as the lawgiver and the keeper thereof, for he shall know that which is ethical and he shall abide thereby. There shall be none among man which shall covet another's possessions, nor shall they be given to know hatred.

THE NEW KINGDOM

IT IS ESTABLISHED THAT THE NEW KINGDOM SHALL BE ESTABLISHED UPON THE "LOTUS" WHICH NOW LIES WITHIN THE BED OF THE PLACE KNOWN AS THE PACIFIC (THE SEA OF PEACE). THERE ARE PORTIONS OF THIS MOTHER COUNTRY WHICH HAS NEVER BEEN SUNKEN BENEATH THE TIDES AND WHICH WILL BLOSSOM IN GLORY AND NEWNESS.

There it will be a time of peace and harmony, and it shall reign for the cycle which shall last for twelve thousand years. Again, she shall be in a new cycle which shall bring another order. Ye have moved forward into her second year in the manner of thy present "timing" Ye would now be at approximate day three hundred seventeen of thy second year of measurement. So be it! For this ending/beginning are the scribes recording for the history is being written as we write upon the pages.

These things coming forth upon thy physical senses shall be as tragedy at the time; yet considering that which is eternal, there must be no "fear" for there is naught such as beginning or ending. The ending of an experience and the beginning anew; what would there be to cause "fear"? I guide of thine way; simply use great wisdom in thy course choice.

Blessed be the man which can be his own strength and stay and calls out unto the Father: "Thy will be done: I am not of the Earth, yet I am cast into it." He shall be in the seeing of the glory of a wondrous dawn; for it is given unto him to know wherein is his strength. He shall not be in the seeking of a place for hiding, but shall go forth to meet that which is apportioned unto him. He shall know truth and it shall most surely give unto him, freedom in magnificence. Not a person shall set foot against his door; not a person shall keep him away from the entering of the Father's house, for by his own hand shall he open all the doors which have been previously shut unto him.

THE LAW

Unto the Father's house from which he went forth, it shall be that he shall triumphantly return. Ah, yes, the Father shall rejoice, for it is given unto Him to wait for His beloved off-spring to go out and again return. Therein, beloved chelas, is WISDOM! It is the Law: so above, so below and for this do they wait that they fulfill the Law which has sent them forth. It is the fulfilling of such Law that they return and that they be made new and groomed for another new and wondrous day; and in that day, they shall know peace and they shall rest from those things which have beleaguered them. So it is ordained. There is naught law of Earth which shall stay the Law which is established unto these things; and so be it and it shall come upon the Earth that which man feareth and that which he cannot comprehend. It will come within thy span and it is at hand.

THE CLARION CALL

Now, again I say unto you which is repeated from the first time of its telling, that which shall be. They have not listened and therefore have not heard the call, nor have they heard the bugle's trumpet which soundeth. IT IS NOT SYMBOLIC BUT IS LITERALLY TRUE; THE CLARION CALL SHALL BE SENT FORTH; THE TRUMPET SHALL BE SOUNDED AND SORROW UNTO THOSE WHO HEED NOT ITS CALL.

There shall be a day when the Sun shall not shine forth; she shall be as a bowl of blood; and she shall give forth no heat. Then, as if in a twinkling of an eye there shall be a great burst of flame which shall be forged from within the Earth herself, and it shall be as the Earth has flipped her axis; and she shall roll and reel and she shall be in the throes of agony. Then the words of comfort shall be spoken which shall settle her down again upon her axis whereby she shall be as a newborn. She shall be as the babe within the bosom of its mother and she shall find comfort and peace. She shall rest.

No man nor woman shall know the hour that this is to come upon the Earth; thereby it is fair warning that ye ones who project in improper knowledge cease and desist from thy false projections for <u>it is not given unto man to know</u>. 'Tis the devil's work that would misguide thee. Know only that there is very little "time" for the fulfillment of these Laws and that which shall come; for it is already written upon the wall and most see of it not for they are as drunken with their own vainglory. They have not seen nor have they listened. Ah, 'tis such the pity, for it is given to man to turn backward and for this does he stumble and fall. So shall he have many injuries and bruises, and no place shall he find rest for his looking only backward, for his looking backward shall bring him much suffering. He can, therefore, be only the bearer of the past; and that is such the pity of it all, for therein is no wisdom.

NOW

From whence came the "past"? From whence came the "present"? And further, from whence might come the "future"? Oh, blessed are the ones who cherish and fortune self for that which is "NOW", FOR IT IS THE ONLY TIME! When this lesson of lessons is well learned, man shall be wise indeed. There is no promise of tomorrow; and the past which is gone shall be always gone. It shall be as the burden upon his back if it be allowed to weigh heavy upon him. With his own hands he must tear the past bundle away from himself and cast it to the winds as dust and chaff from the gleaning centers. Allow the burden to blow away as the dry ash from the soil. Man need not drag his bundle of burdens after them for they shall be given into freedom of all that holds them in bondage, and they too, shall begin in newness.

Beloved ones, it is very near the fulfilling of these things. Look carefully for the signs and signals are all about thee in every direction of thy vision; all facets of projected truth --- IT HAS BEGUN; THY "TIME" HAS TERMINATED.

Dharma, let us leave this now. The lessons are heavy upon the ears and eyes of those who receive. Blessed be thee, child, for the risk is great unto those who dare to pen my truth. Ye are cradled in the security of mine hands and ye shall not fail. Ye ones who bear mine load of preparation are blessed indeed, and thy rewards shall be glory for I cherish ye of mine beloved.

I leave now that ye might find of respite, so be it and selah. I place of mine seal upon these words that no man misunderstand of their definition. IN AND WITHIN GOD THE FATHER CREATOR/CREATION DO I RESIDE AND AS I AM, SO YE ARE AND IT IS SO FOR THUS HAVE I SPOKEN IT UNTO THEE THAT YE MAY REMEMBER.

I AM ESU JESU JESUS SANANDA OF GOD THE TOTALITY

I AM THE SON OF THE GREAT AND SACRED TONKA AND I AM HERE TO STAND BESIDE YE ONES WHO ARE MINE BROTHERS AND SISTERS. SO BE IT AND SELAH.

CHAPTER 11

REC #1 GOD (ATON)

FRIDAY JUNE 30, 1989 6:00 A.M. YEAR 2, DAY 318

I AM ATON, THY SOURCE

I see thee with head bent that thy words be truth; they can be naught but truth for ye have yielded unto me. I AM ATON OF LIGHT. I AM THY SOURCE, CHILD. I HAVE SENT FORTH MINE SONS AND ANGELS UNTO THEE AND I COME FORTH UNTO THEE, LITTLE CHILDREN OF THE UNIVERSE, THAT YOU UNDERSTAND THY TRANSITION.

DO NOT WEEP AT THOSE WHO CHOOSE TO HEAR THEE NOT FOR IT IS ME THEY REFUSE TO HEAR FOR MY SONS AND ANGELS SPEAK IN MINE NAME. THEY ARE THE TRUMPETERS AND CLARIONS OF MY VOICE. I AM THY GOD WITHOUT/WITHIN AND YE ARE BUT ENERGY FRAGMENTS WHICH I HAVE CHOSEN TO GO FORTH AND EXPERIENCE THE UNIVERSE OF MY CREATIONS. UNTO YE ARE GIVEN THE GIFTS OF LIFE AND CREATOR, BUT YE MISUSE OF THE PRECIOUS GIFTS.

<u>LET HIM WHO DARES, TURN HIS FACE FROM MYSELF AND REFUSE THE WORDS OF MINE MESSENGERS. THAT ONE WHO DENIES IS DESTINED TO PROFOUND TRIBULATION. HEED CAREFULLY, CHILDREN OF THE FLESH, YE ARE BUT ENERGY FRAGMENTS IN A PASSING INSTANT OF MINE THOUGHT. HE WHO DENIES TRUTH DENIES ME; HE WHO DENIES ME WILL BE CAST FROM MY THOUGHTS TO EXPERIENCE THE VOID FOR THY PERSECUTIONS OF MINE ONES IS COMING TO TERMINATION IN THY CURRENT TIME. THINK MOST CAREFULLY BEFORE YE PUT TO THE SIDE THESE WORDS FOR THEY ARE MINE WORDS AND AS I CREATE THUSLY I SHALL DISSOLVE. YOUR TIME OF TREMBLING AND TERROR IS CLOSE IN THY TIME. YE ONES OF EARTH WILL HEED MY MESSENGER'S WARNINGS OR THE CONSEQUENCES ARE MIGHTY FOR THAT WHICH HAS BEEN PERPETRATED UPON MINE MAGNIFICENT CREATIONS, IN DARKNESS, SHALL CEASE. IF YOU CHOOSE NOT TO HEAR, YE HAVE CHOSEN THE WAY OF THE VOID AND WILL BE IN PERISHMENT WITHIN THE TIDES AND UPHEAVALS OF LABOR AND BIRTHING. SO IT SHALL BE, THY GAMES OF PUNINESS ARE DRAWING TO A FINISH. I SEAL THESE WORDS THAT YE MIGHT UNDERSTAND THAT YE "WAIT" FOR THAT SPECIAL ONE TO SPEAK FROM "SOMEWHERE" BUT NOT FROM THIS SOURCE; YE ERR GREATLY FOR "I CHOOSE WHO SHALL BE MINE SCRIBES AND BEAR THE BUGLE-------NOT YE ONES."</u>

<u>MOVE OF THY FINGERS, DHARMA, AND CONTINUE THY ALPHABET UPON THE PAGES FOR THIS, MAN HAS WAITED, AND YE FEAR NO MORE FOR THIS IS THY PORTION AND OTHER MAN WILL ACCEPT OR DENY; IT IS FOR HIM TO CHOOSE, YOURS IS TO WRITE. YE ARE IN THE PROTECTION OF MINE ARMY SO PEACE SHALL BE THY GIFT.</u>

YE PLEAD FOR SIGNS

I shall pick up where my Son left off on the yester morn for ye shall not say ye were not told of these things. Ye plead for signs and warnings, timing and reassurance; they are falling all about thine noses----open of thine eyes. Stop thy worry as to whether or not there is "time" to do of thine things----do whatever thee can. It is the foolish waiting when ye know of what ye should do that is thy bother. Turn to thy labors and ye will not note the "waiting".

Within the time which is allotted unto the Earth which is in the present part wherein she is, there shall be a great and mighty change upon her surface and within her bowels. She has been most tormented and active within; she is seething and restless. She is a living, breathing creation who has been badly used. It is not in anger she throws thee from her body but rather, she is in the throes of death from thee. She has carried her burdens in honor and is released therefrom. Instead of moaning about thy displeasures and larking ye had better be in the writing of the new stories to present unto thine brothers. What will be in the second, third and hundredth motion picture? Your purpose is to tell the world my truth that ones can know of their plight. Do ye believe there are no stories within these words? Have ye ones no visions left to serve unto thy brethren? YE CHOOSE TO DENY AND WAIT FOR "PROOF"? SO BE IT --- WAIT. HOWEVER, YE WHO CHOOSE TO TAKE EXCEPTION TO MY WARNINGS AS UNCOMFORTABLE AND PRODDING, TAKE HEED - STOP OF THY WHINING FOR THIS WAS THINE AGREEMENT **WITH ME!** I CARE NOT ONE WHIT WHETHER OR NOT YE LIKE OF MY METHODS OR OF MY SCRIBES. I AM NOT PLEASED WITH YOUR ACTIONS; I WEEP OVER THAT WHICH I HAVE PLACED INTO CREATION THAT HAS DEGRADED AND DEBAUCHED MINE OTHER WONDROUS AND BALANCED ENTITIES. IT IS THY GIFT OF FREEDOM OF CHOICE, FOR I GAVE THAT TOO, UNTO YOU, BUT YE SHALL BEAR THE DIFFICULT ROAD IF YE HEED NOT THE CALL THAT MAKES OF THINE WAY, EASY AND BEAUTEOUS.

Look about thee and see that some things might be in the fitting. For ye have been told that when it is near the fulfilling of these things, it shall be that there shall be great shipwrecks, and the ships of the air and the ships of the sea shall go down. ARE THEY NOT DOING SO? And the fish of the sea shall seek new places wherein to spawn. ARE THEY NOT DOING SO, FROM THY POLLUTION AND FUEL SPILLINGS?

AND -- THERE SHALL APPEAR UPON THE EARTH NEW PEOPLE WHICH ARE **NOT INDIGENOUS OF THE EARTH**, AND THAT WHICH HAS NOT BEEN SEEN BEFORE. YE HAD BETTER TAKE NOTE; STOP OF THY DENIAL AND WELCOME THY SIBORS, CHELAS --- YE ARE IN GRAVE CIRCUMSTANCE AND I HAVE SENT MINE OTHER CHILDREN OF THE UNIVERSE AND THE VERY ANGELS OF MY REALMS TO ASSIST YE. REFUSE THEM IF YE CHOOSE BUT **KNOW 'TIS YOU WHO HAVE REFUSED.** WALK WITH MY CHILDREN AND THY NEW SIBORS AND YE SHALL WALK IN GLORY. THEY ARE COME TO SHOW YOU THE WAY; MY SONS HAVE COME AGAIN TO RECLAIM MINE HOUSES.

THY MOTHER EARTH HAS SUFFERED ENOUGH

Thy very Earth Source has been seized with convulsions within her entrails, and she has belched forth that which is from within her interior --- and, these things shall increase and increase. She has been in such great pain for such a great time, for thy Mother Earth that she is, is not without great travail. Oh, and such is the pity of it, for man has been unmindful of her; and as she has nurtured him, fed him, clothed him and mothered him, he has remained more and more unmindful of her --- he has been unto her a carnal and lecherous son. I RECOGNIZE, IN HONOR, THOSE WHO HAVE CHANGED OF THEIR LASCIVIOUS WAYS AND NOW REACH OUT TO ASSIST. BEWARE, HOWEVER, OF THOSE WHO FORM "MOVEMENTS" IN FALSE INTENT. **KNOW OF THAT WHICH YE CHOOSE PARTICIPATION.** Man has been much like the salamanders and moles who burrow within her body and has taken and taken from her and given nothing in return. He is blind in his licentiousness, for he has had no thought given of that which has nursed him and healed of his injuries and infirmities.

So be it that he has but added suffering unto insults which have been given unto the Mother Earth wherein man has had his birth into the physical parts of me. And therein is great commiseration of him which is in darkness. They see not with the eyes which are blindfolded, but they see only that which is unreal, unholy and filled with greed; for I am whole and I can see that which is wondrously complete, and I have not want for I am unto myself all that of which I have need.

I AM THE CREATOR

In this time of casting off I rejoice that I shall make myself into newness for I represent the Creation of Earth for I become one with my creations and ye have forgotten. Unto this end do I create. I have brought up races of men that they might become Gods and that they might become wise creators also, and that they might become one with myself. This is every man's inheritance. Man shall be in no wise the poorer for having experienced in his growth. I am the Creator and I have created wisely, though I often weep at thine poor choices; and, I have sent man into all the worlds wherein there is life, and oh, precious ones, there are many! All who have gone forth from me have returned unto me richer and more glorious for their experiences.

There is naught place wherein is the form of man wherein is not the parts of Me. I have divided myself into parts, and I have endowed each part with the part of myself, that which is eternal - infinite -, and that part of Me changes not but remains ever unchanged by anything which is or shall ever be.

In my own timing shall I bring them all in again, to become again one with Me and they shall all be made whole. From the body of myself have I created all things, both of the land and of the sea, and of the air; and therein are the things, both of land and sea, and the words become manifest. The things which I command appear, and they take form, and then I breathe into them, life. They are the animated parts of Me; and they cannot be less than the Gods, because I have created each after a likeness which I have conceived within my own being. It is the positive that I am, and creation is the negative.

That part which ye "see" is the part of Me which is subject to change and which shall return to the elements from which it came. Not a person shall change the Law, nor shall he bring unto me one part of himself which is of the earth; for I bring back unto Me that which is eternal, and that which is of the earth I shake off. It gives Me great joy to bring back that which I send out for it is this for which I have made provision.

Positive/ negative, night/day, ah yes, there are two poles of force called "life", as in darkness and light, soul/spirit and body, LIFE AND DEATH. Many are the labels placed upon the positive and negative; yet there is only **ONE** AND THAT **ONE** IS ALL INCLUSIVE, FOR IT IS OF MYSELF AND FROM MYSELF THAT I HAVE CREATED ALL THINGS, AND FROM **ONE SUBSTANCE** HAVE ALL THINGS COME INTO BEING.

WE SHALL AGAIN BE ONE

So shall man learn these things of Me for they shall be made to sit in the council with Me and we shall again be ONE.

There shall come forth a new order upon the Earth, for I have created wisely, and when a portion of myself offends me, I cast it off and I begin anew. I shall bind up mine wounds and I shall heal myself, and I shall be as whole again. It is not with pity for myself, but that which I have created, that they know not that which they cut themselves off from, nor do they know their own identity. For this do I weep; for they have blasphemed and been disrespectful unto Me and unto mine other creations.

I have wept that I have created man, for he has become foul, and has become so often as the stench of the Earth; he has poisoned his own food; and he has given unto his brother the potion of the asps; and he has been unto himself renegade, for he has not kept his covenant with Me. Most often he has not been an honor unto me upon the Earth. As I sent him forth he was perfect but he has ceased his perfection upon mine Earth globe. He has committed all of the forbidden crimes against Earth and brother and has become blind as the creatures that burrow in the ground or live within the darkened caves. I am most often given into shame for that which I created and placed, as man, upon Earth -- -- yet, beloved of mine, I love without limits that which errs, for that too, is my creation and 'tis for him I created and sent him forth.

In due time he shall be purified with fire, and he shall return unto me as the SONS OF GOD. There shall then be much rejoicing, for it shall be as nothing man has ever experienced, for there shall be much ecstatic rejoining and alas, much weeping; for it is given unto man to be purified by his tears and his sorrows. So be it that he shall have them so he may know joy. Ah, chelas, in this there truly is wisdom.

I say that I am his joy and I am his tears, and by his tears shall he come to know me. With my own hand shall I then wipe away the tears from his face that he has shed in my name and for my sake. He shall then be whole.

HOW IT WILL BE

Beloved, the events will not be stayed for actually, it is finished. When it shall come upon the Earth that which shall be, it is said that there shall be great suffering, and there shall be. Of all things, the fire and the wind shall be worse, for it shall be mighty spouts of fire and molten lava from the pits of Earth, and it shall be liquid and white with heat, and the winds shall fan it and it shall not cool, nor shall they put out the fire, for it shall burn as it touches, and it shall scorch the Earth for miles --- and it shall have enormous velocity. With the blowing winds it shall be flung unto widespread portions of the countrysides. Those who recognize and have builded their hovels against that day can be shielded from the rain of burning fragments but the hovels must be built above the flows in those places near the cinder cones. Thy Mother is releasing the eons of stored corruption from within. The pressures are beyond your ability to measure. It shall be thus in the places where ye are, chela, for I speak now of thy locale for there are others who will speak of other.

There shall, within a short duration of time from the first, another within the place where is now the Ocean of Peace (Pacific), and a third within another shorter period of time, within the eastern part of the Atlantic Ocean (the places of Atlantis); and it shall not be within the confines of the land which is above the water. It shall force that which is now the bottom of the Atlantic to the surface of the water and there to tower far above and beyond. Go forth and tell mine children how it will be for it will be given unto you to make wondrous visions that they might see and know of these things which will come. Ye will be shown the methods and given unto you that which is needed; my creatures must be informed and given expectation. So be it. Ye who think ye cannot write, go within and pen that which is shown unto thee. Paint the visions for those who have no vision for I shall hold my wrath until warning might go forth. I plead with you, little ones, to heed the assistance of thy brethren whom I have sent unto you.

THE LIGHT AND THE LAW

I AM THE LIGHT AND THE LAW AND I WILL SPEAK UPON THESE THINGS.

It is fortuned unto man to be within the Law, yet he has chosen to not be a worker within the Light. With the Light which is given unto him he has been thoughtless of his Source and his ONENESS with ME. He has cast himself into utter darkness and degradations while writhing in carnal activities within the great cities having been trapped by the Satanic tentacles of the lie.

Now I say unto you that all might come to know in this time at hand. He shall come to be most mindful of this Source and this, within this time, for ye are only in the beginning. Thy present generation will see and experience these things come to pass as projected by the great and humble prophets sent to prepare thee.

There will come forth a loud cry for peace and man shall frantically seek and search for balance and peace. Some who seek will find it for they will look upon truth; others will not find it for they will accept the lies and call the truth -- "lie". So be it and I speak, for to them which find it shall be delivered up, and they shall be placed within safety where abides peace.

BACK TO SQUARE ONE

Unto those which find not peace, they shall be put into a place wherein they may labor for their bread and wherein they begin anew.

They shall have for their tools only their bare hands for they shall be again as in the beginning. They shall learn that which is Lawful and that which is profitable unto them; that which is of the eternal. Again, they will not, from the onset, be given to remember their past, nor will they know of their future. So shall they work from day unto day in blindness; for it is the Law that "EVERY MAN UNTO HIS OWN" and with his own hands shall he build up his temple or tear of it down. (Might this sound as a "rerun of the play" to ye chelas who are coming into knowledge and truth?) Rejoice ye ones who have seen the way. I say rejoice!

Now I say unto you again, for I said it once before unto my scribes, they shall be as the beasts of the fields, for they have not prepared for the day when they shall be brought in. They have wasted their inheritance and have been unto themselves, betrayers. Oh, beloved ones, the compassion is beyond endurance but so shall it be for all will mature and learn that they might walk in the presence, one with Me. For man will either have chosen the way of the Law or he will have chosen to walk in separation with the fallen angels.

FOR THOSE WHO SEE THE LIGHT

For those which have been mindful of the Law and the Light, and worked therein, they shall be brought into a place of newness wherein is total light. They shall be relieved of all stresses, for it is Lawful to say that they shall be brought into the place wherein I AM; for I have prepared for them a place and I have provided well; and for this day I have provided. At no time do I forget the "little ones" in darkness, for I have reached out within the darkness for them and they have turned away and denied of me and of my messengers.

NOT A PERSON SHALL DENY THAT THIS IS SO! THEY HAVE BEEN MOST FOOLISH. SO BE IT AS IT MAY BE, I HAVE NOT FORGOTTEN THEM IN THEIR SLUMBERS YET AND IN THEIR DRUNKENNESS. THEY DO NOT YET REMEMBER FROM WHENCE THEY CAME, NOR DO THEY YET KNOW WHITHER THEY GOEST. I SEND THEE THAT YE MIGHT TELL THEM-------THE ULTIMATE CHOICE WILL REST WITH EACH. SO BE IT FOR IT IS SO AND I GIVE UNTO THESE WORDS THE SEAL WHICH IS OF GOD FOR IT SHALL COME TO PASS IN THIS MANNER AS I HAVE GIVEN IT UNTO THEE. THE TIME HAS COME TO RISE FROM THY BEDDINGS AND CHOOSE OF THY PATH LEST YE CHOOSE WRONGLY. I AWAIT THEE FOR THE FINAL CURTAIN OF THIS CYCLE IS READY TO FALL -- FOR EVER. I CALL UPON YOU TO TAKE THE OFFERED HAND OF THY BRETHREN WHO HAVE AGAIN COME AMONG YOU TO LEAD THEE HOME.

I URGE YOU TO TAKE GREAT CAUTION; I AM THY GOD, YE TURN FROM MY MESSENGERS AND MINE SONS SENT FORTH AGAIN UNTO YOU AND DENY THESE WORDS AND YE ERR BEYOND THY COMPREHENSION. SO BE IT.

I AM

Go, Dharma, for ye have finished of thy work this morning. Man must digest a bit of the lead and denial he will be feeling from the words; he has but a short time to be in the deciding. The years dwindle down to such a precious few -- even in thy physical time frames. Do not depress yourself as thy job is well done and I cherish of thee for thy faithfulness. Go and rest and allow of the energy to settle and calm; ye are in the care of my most beloved Son in whom I continually rejoice. I place mine hand upon thy head in blessings, ye who stand with me.

EPILOG

I am Gyeorgos Ceres Hatonn, Commander in Chief, Earth Project Transition, Pleiades Sector Flight Command, Intergalactic Federation Fleet-Ashtar Command; Earth Representative to the Cosmic Council and Intergalactic Federation Council on Earth Transition. You may call me "Hatonn".

Let there be no misunderstanding of WHO I AM! I come in this portion as a fourth dimensional Project Commander in charge of Earth Transition. As this is most thoroughly explained in other recordings from myself and others, I shall not cover it in this document.

This document contains truth which can be validated. It comes forth in dictated format from myself to one of my transreceivers (recorder). There is nothing of "channeling" about it - it is via actual radio type short wave directly from my source into a receiver terminal. No hocus pocus nor mystical hoopla. This recorder does exactly that --- records. She is not privy to the information resources nor is she given to "interpretation" other than as any other reader would personally interpret.

We, of the lighted brotherhood of the Cosmic and Galactic participants are ready to make our presence upon your place. We travel and act in the direct service and under Command of Esu Jesus Immanuel Sananda. Sananda is aboard my Command Craft from whence He will direct all evacuation and transition activities as regards the period you ones call the End Prophecies of Armageddon.

He has organized placement for His peoples and will oversee all operations as regards His people. All Intergalactic Fleets are under His command, and for purposes of evacuation, those details are in most capable hands of one called, simply, Commander Ashtar.

There will be more and more frequent contact with ones of human format by ones of our commands. You will ask any energy form contacting you, to identify. Demand that if the energy is not of the "light" of the Divine Source to remove itself. DO NOT ENTERTAIN ANY/AND ALL ENERGY FRAGMENTS WHO APPEAR TO YOU FOR MORE AND MORE OF THE DARK ENERGY FORMS ARE MAKING CONTACT.

EXTREME CAUTION: DO NOT RUN AND HOP ABOARD ANY SPACE CRAFT WHICH MIGHT LAND -- CAUSE THE ENTITIES TO IDENTIFY THEMSELVES. INSTRUCTIONS FOR IDENTIFICATION OF THE INTERGALACTIC COMMANDS ARE BEING PRESENTED CURRENTLY AND WILL BE FORTHCOMING IN A MASSIVE WAY VERY SHORTLY.

This document is for the purpose of awakening you to the horrendous lie that has been perpetrated against you ones. I am giving it to insure protection of those human ones who dared bring it into the open and yet risk their lives having done so. I dedicate it to the ones who dared and have been mocked, ridiculed and persecuted for having dared to give you help to "save" yourselves from the lies. I go on record to my adversaries herewith and place them on formal notice: YE SHALL NOT BRING HARM UNTO MY WORKERS, NOR UNTO THEIR COWORKERS, FAMILIES OR FRIENDS ATTACHED THERETO.

Now, I shall tell you who I am in my Higher Command. I AM ATON. Perhaps you might wish to look up that label for it might prove to be quite important to you. I shall see to it that these instructions are carried forth, so I suggest there be no toying with this as some game of sorts to be discounted at your next little seminar gathering of the flying saucer clubs and crystal worshipers. Your time of playing at star readings, Ouija boards and Taro, to seek your fortunes, is over.

Earth is going to plod right through evolution, transition, tribulation, new "birthing" and new "berthing" just as written. You need no psychic reader to tell you how it will be. You can hide your head in your sand bucket; it will change nothing.

There are detailed and magnificent plans in operation to cause the transition to be quite survivable and workable for those of you who so choose to work with us and not in the enemy camp. The Evil Forces shall be met and stopped but it will be a most unpleasant confrontation.

The Master Esu Jesus Immanuel Sananda is returned and awaits the appointed time. If you want information I suggest heartily that you contact A.S.S.K. for any and all information. We will be printing it in numerous volumes as fast as our scribes can receive.

I dedicate this work to all who have taken a stand for truth. I also dedicate it to our beloved Sister Thedra who has labored day and night as a hand scribe to beloved Sananda for over forty years.

And of course, my infinite love and appreciation to Dharma, who works hours each and every day in our service. This is but a tiny portion of her works. I so honor my small circle who are in the building of physical foundations and yet also see to it that these words are carried forth in truth and dispersment. Also to those who give such unselfish support in so many other ways without which help we could not proceed. Blessings be yours, little ones, as ye are cherished beyond thy ability to comprehend. I so look forward to the day I can give you public credit for your service and yet allow for your security. Know that your names are written on the tablets of the Book of Life. There shall, however, come the day when you shall have thy works made known unto thy fellow men.

I request this book be brought to the public with all haste for the physical protection of some of thy brothers rests heavily upon its promptness.

I PLACE MY SEAL UPON THESE WRITINGS OF TRUTH. YOU ONES MUST AWAKEN NOW FOR YOU HAVE SLEPT TOO LONG AND YOUR WORLD IS CRUMBLING DOWN AROUND THY FEET. YOU ARE IN THE FINAL COUNTDOWN.

I AM ATON

AUGUST 31, 1989
DAY 016, YEAR 3

This reproduction is from an actual photograph taken on June 1st, 1961, in Chichen Itza, Yucatan, by one of thirty archaeologists working in the area at the time. Sananda appeared in visible, tangible body and permitted His photograph to be taken.

GOBOX

GOBOX CONTENTS

The DYNAMO Radio with AM/FM. Flash light, built-in nicad rechargeable battery with AC/DC adaptor (Optional). Built-in hand cranked generator that recharges the battery. All-In-One-Tool (Hammer, hatchet, saw, shovel, nail puller & bottle opener). 36 hearty ready to eat meals, HOT OR COLD, stove, bowls, tumblers, utensils, water purifier, 1st aid kit, matches, detergent, toilet tissue & towels.

THE MOST COMPLETE 72 HOUR EMERGENCY KIT AVAILABLE FOR A FAMILY OF FOUR. ALL YOU NEED TO GO WITH THE GOBOX IS YOUR PERSONAL ITEMS, SLEEPING GEAR AND APPROXIMATELY 3 GALLONS OF WATER.

The GOBOX is designed for immediate evacuation, just GRAB IT and go. KEEP one "HANDY" at home, in your car, camper, boat, or airplane, along with the water (PROPERLY PACKAGED).

RETAIL PRICE--------------------------------------$149.95
CLUB MEMBERSHIP PRICE-----------------------------$109.95
Plus shipping costs. Utah residents add $6.88 sales tax.

ROSS PACKING, INC
2300 E Ave
OGDEN, UTAH 84401
801 392-3515

REFERRALS

ADDITIONAL SOURCE INFORMATION:

PHYSICAL SURVIVAL INFORMATION:

Merlin B. Sampson
NATIONAL BUYING CLUB
P.O. Box 396
Midvale, Utah 84047
801 561-5615

CORPORATIONS INFORMATION:

Harley Laughlin
LAUGHLIN ASSOCIATES, INC.
1000 East William St. Ste. 100
Carson City, Nevada 89701
800 648-0966

OR

E.J. EKKER
21512 Adam Dr. #3093 B
Tehachapi, California 93561-9802
805 822-0601